# THE KINGFISHER BOOK OF
# MUSIC

KINGFISHER
An imprint of Larousse plc
Elsley House, 24–30 Great Titchfield Street,
London W1P 7AD

First published in 1996 by Kingfisher

10 9 8 7 6 5 4 3 2 1

A CIP catalogue record for this book is available from the
British Library.

ISBN 1 85697 338 7

Editor: Clive Wilson
Designer: Tracy Killick
Authors: Nicky Barber, Mark Barratt,
Alan Blackwood, Elinor Kelly, Chris de Souza
Consultant: Avril Thompson
Picture research: Elaine Willis, Su Alexander,
Image Select (London)
Cover design: Mike Davis
Indexer: Stuart Dunlop and Kay Wright
Photographer: Tim Ridley
Researcher: Laura Sheppard

Colour separation by Newsele s.r.l. Milan, Italy
Printed in Singapore

# THE KINGFISHER BOOK OF
# MUSIC

Kingfisher

# *Foreword*

I was extremely lucky, in the early years of my life, to be a beneficiary of the great teaching tradition which continues to this day at the Liszt Academy in Budapest. Among my teachers was Zoltán Kodály, whose own teaching method, which encourages music making from a child's earliest years, has now influenced three generations of young people all over the world.

Good music, of all kinds, enriches our lives immeasurably and I believe it is never too early to start the process of music education and encourage a love of music in our children.

A book such as this is an invaluable first introduction to music and musicians. I particularly welcome its recognition that music belongs to every corner of the world and I hope that its pages will provide enjoyment and inspiration to young people for many years to come.

Georg Solti

# Contents

F Indicates a feature spread

# How to Use this Book

**Music notation** appears throughout the book. To find out more about these symbols see the *Music to the Ears* chapter and the *Glossary*.

**A history picture** introduces the main topic covered by the spread. It appears in the top left hand corner of each page.

*The Kingfisher Book of Music* has many features that help you explore the fascinating world of music. There are over 250 colour photographs and illustrations to complement the informative text. Time lines show what was happening in the arts, sciences, history and music during a particular period. Mini globes pinpoint the location of different musical traditions across the world, while listening guides highlight essential pieces. The feature spreads give an insider's view on four fascinating subjects – Indian classical dance, buildings for music, the life and times of Ludwig van Beethoven and the musical, *West Side Story*. At the back you will find a reference section. This includes a glossary that explains many of the terms used in the book. These two pages show you how to get the most out of *The Kingfisher Book of Music*.

**The main text** examines fascinating topics from almost every area of music.

**Illustrated boxes** contain additional in-depth information.

**The time line** runs throughout the chapter called *Music in Time and Place*. It tells you, at a glance, important achievements in music, the arts, sciences and exploration and major historical events relating to the spread.

**Symbols** identify each event in the time line –
♪ Music
☞ Historical events
♀ Science and exploration
🎭 The arts

MUSIC IN TIME AND PLACE

## The Middle Ages

The Middle Ages span almost a thousand years of European history. They began with the break-up of the western Roman Empire in the AD470s and ended in the 1400s when some of the countries we know today were beginning to take shape. In the early Middle Ages, the Christian church began to develop a type of music known as plainsong. Based on ancient Jewish chanting, this music was sung in unison and without any accompanying instruments.

In about AD1000 Guido d'Arezzo, a Benedictine monk, invented staff notation. This way of writing down music had a major impact on the way music was sung. Western music moved away from its Middle Eastern origins and developed harmony, writing two or more notes to be played together in the form of chords. In the mid-1300s Guillaume de Machaut was celebrated for the harmonies and beauty of his music. For the first time, composers were recognized as artists with their own individual style.

△ In this illuminated manuscript from the 1070s, King David plucks a harp. Below him a minstrel plays a rebec, an early ancestor of the violin.

▽ *Summer is coming in*, an English song composed around 1310, celebrates the end of winter. The words are written in English and Latin.

△ Guido d'Arezzo, shown here on the left, invented staff notation. This way of writing down notes is still used today.

### WANDERING MUSICIANS

Outside the Church, a whole range of non-religious music was performed during the Middle Ages. From about AD1000 students known as Goliards began to wander from court to court across Europe reciting poetry and songs. Jongleurs were travelling performers who entertained audiences in towns and villages with musical performances, juggling and acrobatic feats. During the late 1100s and 1200s, poet-musicians called troubadours sang tales of courtly love and chivalry. Many troubadours were knights and noblemen.

◁ In the Middle Ages, Christians believed that the end of the world would be heralded in by angels blowing trumpets. This picture was painted in Germany during the 1400s.

### TIME LINE

☞ **476** End of the Roman Empire in Europe
♪ **590-600** Gregory I makes collection of plainsong
🎭 **698** Lindisfarne Gospel, produced in England
♪ **750s** Wind organs first developed
☞ **800** Charlemagne becomes first Holy Roman Emperor
🎭 **800s** Romanesque style of architecture emerges in Europe
♪ **c.1000** Guido d'Arezzo's invents staff notation
☞ **1066** William of Normandy becomes King of England
♪ **1120s** Rise of troubadours, France
♪ **1150** Notre Dame School of Music is founded
🎭 **1230** Gothic cathedral of Chartres, France, is completed
♀ **1276** First paper mill built, in Italy
♪ **c.1250** Motet form of singing develops
♪ **1350** Clavichord, an early keyboard instrument, invented
🎭 **1386-1400** Chaucer's *Canterbury Tales* written

34

35

MUSIC IN TIME AND PLACE

## Indi

Mus for t the The be

o K c M fo

BHA

△ Rama grieving over the loss of Sita

△ Ravana, the evil demon king

22

**Labels** help pinpoint the main details on the larger images.

**Side panels** illustrate one special aspect of the feature spreads.

**The feature spreads** take an in-depth look at particular subjects. You can identify them by their pale blue pages and large, detailed illustrations.

**Listen for** panels highlight some of the best-known pieces of music associated with particular instruments.

**Colour photographs and illustrations** bring the featured subject vividly to life.

**Exploded illustrations** in the *Instruments* chapter show the parts that make up the instrument and how the pieces fit together.

## ical Dance

een an important part of Indian culture
any of the dances have close links with
are inspired by its myths and legends.
e stories as well as tales of epic battles
ons.
ance developed in the various regions
emerged from the temples in the south.
ced only by men,
the south-west.
, is similar to
while *Manipuri*
the north-east.

▷ The tinkling sound from an anklet of tiny bells draws attention to the dancer's legs and feet. Most Indian dance is performed barefoot.

l temple
ument.
*sangita*
ncing.

*Jingles ring out as dancer moves*

Indian classical dancers are among the most graceful in the world. Their gestures and poses convey a wide range of emotions. The body is divided into major sections (*anga*) of the head, torso, arms and legs. Minor sections (*upanga*), include the angle of the nose and chin, and movements of the eyes.

*Right hand represents Rama's bow*

▷ Hand and finger positions, called *mudras*, are a very expressive part of Indian dance. *Bharat Natya* has over 50 different hand and finger postions.

▽ Tying a garland of flowers

▽ A flower blossoming

▽ Pointing to the Moon

▽ Krishna playing the flute

▽ Stroking a cow

▽ A bee landing on a flower

*Left hand represents Rama's arrows*

*Pose represents Rama, the great hunter*

◁ A *Bharat Natya* dancer depicts the god Rama. She is showing Rama holding a bow in one hand and arrows in the other. This is the oldest type of Indian classical dance. It is a dance only performed by women.

◁ Sita lighting her lamp

◁ Poses in the *Bharat Natya* dance drama tell the story of Rama and Sita, two of the gods of Hindu mythology who faced many perils together. Other gods and demons are also portrayed in this dance.

▽Vishnu, the supreme god

◁ King Dasaratha, Rama's father

*Feet stamp out rhythm*

*Ankle bells*

## Trombones and Trumpets

The shrill sound of the trumpet has long been used to send signals and messages, to frighten enemies in battle and to celebrate rituals and ceremonies. The sound of conch shell trumpets was heard by Captain Cook as he approached the islands of Hawaii in the Pacific. The islanders were trying to scare off his ships with their wild noises! The Romans also knew the value of the trumpet – especially in war. They used a long trumpet called a *cornu* both to direct the movements of their own troops and to strike fear in the enemy.

The trombone first appears in European paintings from about 1460. Early trombones in England were known as sackbuts. Apart from a wider bore and a different mouthpiece, the trombone has changed very little over the centuries. Today, the trombone has a regular place in marching bands, orchestras and in jazz music.

△ A wooden angel trumpeter outside St David's cathedral, South Wales.

▽ The modern trumpet has three piston valves. Its length of tubing is curled in on itself to make it easier to carry and play.

*Piston valves*

*Tuning slide changes pitch*

*Cup-shaped mouthpiece*

*Water key releases build-up of condensation*

*Flared bell*

*Counterweight balances instrument*

*Barrel contains spring to cushion impact of slide*

*Tuning slide bow*

*Brace for left hand*

◁ The trombone is different from all the other brass instruments in that it has a slide. The player pushes and pulls the slide to change the length of tubing, which in turn changes the pitch.

*Mouthpiece*

*Water key*

*Inner tube of slide made of hard-wearing alloy*

*Slide brace for right hand*

*Outer tube of slide made of thin brass*

*Bumper knob protects tubing*

▽ This wooden trumpet comes from Papua New Guinea. The musician blows into the hole bored in its side.

**BRASS FAMILY**

trombone          trumpet

trumpet

trombone

The trumpet usually played in bands and orchestras is the B(flat) trumpet. The trombone section usually includes two tenor trombones and one bass trombone.

◁ The didgeridoo makes a deep, droning sound and is played by the Aborigine of Australia. The player must breath in through the hole while blowing down the hollowed out instrument

▽ American trumpeter Miles Davis (1926–1991) was one of the most inventive jazz musicians of all time. He developed bebop and jazz fusion which combined jazz with rock.

82                                                                                          83

**Captions** give details about the illustrations and photographs.

**Pitch and position** boxes show where an instrument is played in the orchestra. They also show the relative sizes of instruments from the same family, as well as the highest and lowest notes that each one can play.

**Famous musicians** are shown playing their instruments throughout the *Instruments* chapter.

# A World of Music

▽ Jazz has its roots in the southern part of North America. You can read about this explosive mixture of African rhythms and European harmony on pages 50–51. Discover the musical heritage of Native Americans on pages 30–31.

▷ Classical music in Europe has a long and fascinating history. Its story is told on pages 34–49.

▷ The catchy rhythms of Latin American music have conquered the world of dancing. Much older still are the panpipes which have been played in South America for thousands of years. To find out more turn to pages 28-29.

▷ Africa has an amazing range of instruments, including many made from gourds, or dried vegetables. To read about these and other fascinating instruments from around the world turn to pages 58–89.

All over the world, people play and listen to music. There are as many kinds of music as there are peoples and places. In every corner of the globe, music plays an important part in peoples' lives, in religious worship, as entertainment, as a means of communication or simply as an enjoyable pastime.

◁ Japan is the birthplace of the compact disc. You can find out about music and recording on pages 100–101.

▷ The Sydney Opera House is one of the world's most famous landmarks. Other buildings for music are revealed on pages 102–103. Australia is also home to the Aborigine people who have used songs and music for over 40,000 years. The music of Australia and Oceania is explored on pages 16–17.

# Sounds and Notes

Sound is energy in the form of vibrations called soundwaves. A plucked string, for example, starts the air vibrating. Our eardrums pick up the movements and our brain interprets them as sounds. A musical note is made when a vibration is steady.

Notes can be organized in scales running from low to high. Different scales have been used at different times in history and vary enormously around the world. Western scales have eight notes. Each set of eight notes is called an octave. Scales made up of five notes are used in Chinese, Celtic, Inuit and African music. Notes are separated by 'intervals' and these also vary around the world. An interval is the distance in pitch between one note and another. The quivering feel to some Indian or Chinese music is because the interval between each note is very tiny. The notes of Indian scales are arranged in traditional patterns called *ragas* which represent different emotions and moods.

Musical sounds can be long or short, loud or quiet. They also vary in 'tone'. This is the quality that makes our voices and instruments sound different from each other.

△ A medieval manuscript showing the philosophers Pythagoras (top right) and Boethius (top left). Through experiments and theory they laid the foundations for today's system of notes and scales.

△ A scale is a number of notes, ascending or descending in 'steps'. There is a fixed interval between each step. The Western scale is made up of eight notes, seven of which are named A to G. The eighth, or finishing note, has the same letter as the starting note. Here the scale of C is shown.

*Treble clef*

*Middle C in the treble clef*

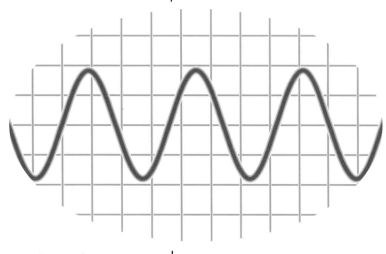

△ A sound wave shown on an instrument called an oscilloscope. The speed of the wave determines the sound's pitch. The depth determines the sound's loudness.

**Outer ear**

**Middle ear**

**Cochlea**

*Auditory nerve to the brain*

▷ The outer part of the ear funnels sound waves towards the eardrum, which in turn vibrates. These vibrations are passed to the spiral-shaped cochlea in the inner ear. Electrical pulses are then sent along the auditory nerve to the brain. Finally, the brain interprets these pulses as sound.

**Ear passage**

**Eardrum**

**Inner ear**

◁ Concorde, the world's only commercial supersonic aeroplane, demonstrates the power of sound. At close range the noise from its engines can easily burst a person's eardrums.

▽ The piano keyboard is arranged with the lowest or deepest notes on the left, and the highest notes on the right. The letters on the keys correspond to the notes on the stave of music (left). They show two octaves in the scale of C major.

**Stave**

*Middle C*

# Music's Heartbeat

Music without rhythm would be like a person without a backbone. It would collapse in a heap. Rhythm is nearly always a regular pulse or beat, usually easy to tap the foot to, or to dance to. Like the ticking of a clock, it marks the passage of time.

This rhythmic pulse or beat is measured in regular sections called bars. Various types of music have their own number of beats to the bar. This is written down in two numbers at the beginning of the piece of music, and is called the time signature. The top number tells you how many beats are in each bar. The bottom one shows you how long each beat lasts. The waltz has three beats to the bar, while most rock music has four beats to the bar.

Different countries and cultures have their own rhythms. African music has complex rhythms created by mixing a variety of drum and bell beats or handclapping. African rhythms combined with American band traditions and European harmonies form the basis for jazz. Native American music has two separate rhythms, one for the drums and one for vocals.

△ The beating of drums is one of the oldest and most widespread forms of music. These Persian women are dancing to the rhythmic sound of the drums.

▷ The metronome produces a ticking sound. It can be set at different speeds, or 'tempi', according to the metronome mark on the music. The steady tick helps the practising musician keep to the correct beat.

▷ As well as drums, the North African Berbers make use of a lot of handclapping. Clapping to a beat expresses our feeling for rhythm in the most natural way.

△ Many rhythms in and around the Sahara Desert are based on the steady tread of the camel.

▷ Much of the energy of rock music comes from the power of the drumming. Included in this musician's drum kit are two snare drums, a floor tom, a bass drum and three cymbals. These are played with drumsticks or wire brushes.

**TIME VALUES**

*Semibreve*

*Rests*

*Minim*

*Crotchet*

*Quaver*

*Semiquaver*

*Tied notes*

Notes and rests are given different lengths, or time values. The notes and rests shown here are each half the length of the note or rest above them. The two time signatures below indicate the number and type of notes to the bar.

*Duple time*

$\frac{2}{4}$

*Triple time*

$\frac{3}{4}$

# Writing Music Down

△ Japanese *koto* music uses the *Ikuta* system of notation. Reading down each column indicates which strings are to be played as well as the basic beat.

Most cultures have developed their own musical systems. Not all, however, place great importance on writing music down. Much non-Western music – as well as some Western music – is passed from person to person simply by being listened to and repeated. This can make music feel alive and vibrant. It can also, unfortunately, lead to the loss of very beautiful pieces.

The best-known method of writing music is Western notation. Notes are written on a set of five lines, called a stave, and placed higher or lower according to their pitch. By describing the length of each note or rest, it also shows rhythm. Other words or signs tell the musician whether he or she should play loudly or softly, lively or smoothly.

Each piece of music has a shape. Just like a story, the composer gives it a beginning, a middle and an end. Written music draws our attention to this structure, showing how basic tunes or rhythms are repeated or developed.

△ Jazz musicians improvising. Despite notation, a good deal of music has always been improvised – that is, made up on the spur of the moment. The musicians start with a tune or rhythm, developing it as the mood builds up.

## MUSIC NOTATION

Clef signs (right) appear at the beginning of each line of a piece of music. They indicate the pitch of all the notes as they are written down on the stave. There are four types of clef – treble, alto, tenor and bass.

A triad (lower right) is a basic three note chord. A scale consists of the successive notes of a key. Sharps and flats (below) raise or lower the pitch of a note by a semi-tone. A natural sign cancels them out.

Treble clef

Alto clef

Tenor clef

Bass clef

Triads

Scale of F major — *b flat*

Scale of G major — *f sharp*

Accidentals

♯ Sharp

𝄪 Double sharp

♭ Flat

𝄫 Double flat

♮ Natural

△ A beautiful example of medieval Western notation. The pitched notes of the melody are positioned on the stave and the words of the song written underneath. A more primitive system of 'neumes', which reminded the singer of the tune's 'shape', existed as early as the 600s.

>A range of ideas lies behind every musical performance. The Chinese musical system has as its foundation a single note, or 'yellow bell'. From this a series of twelve notes was born, linked with the hours of the day and the months of the year.

# Oceania and Australia

Scattered across the deep waters of the Pacific Ocean are thousands of islands whose musical traditions are closely bound up with the sea. The people who live in this region, known as Oceania, once travelled from island to island by canoe. They took drums, flutes and pipes with them and settled on islands such as Papua New Guinea and Hawaii. Their music still includes chants to help them navigate.

Thought to be one of the oldest peoples in the world, the Aborigines first came to Australia 50,000 years ago. Like the peoples of Oceania, a great deal of their music relies on the voice and natural sounds such as hand-clapping and foot-stamping. Many of their songs and dances tell how the earth was created. These rituals, as well as their musical instruments, have probably not changed much in tens of thousands of years.

△ Music, singing and dancing have always been central to the Australian Aborigine's way of life. This cave painting shows figures playing the didgeridoo and performing a ceremonial dance.

△ At a ceremonial dance in Papua New Guinea, the rhythm is maintained by a *kundu* (hourglass) drum. The music of this island includes warlike chanting and yodelling as well as more gentle flute and drum music.

◁ The didgeridoo is made from tree branches hollowed out by termites. Traditionally only men were allowed to play this sacred Aboriginal instrument.

## THE BULL-ROARER

The bull-roarer has been used for more than 25,000 years by peoples around the world. Usually made of wood and attached to a length of cord, it makes a screaming sound when spun through the air. The decorations on this bull-roarer from Papua New Guinea are believed to have magical powers that can drive out evil spirits.

▷ The chants and shouts of the New Zealand Maori war dance, or *haka*, are also accompanied with foot stamping and unusual facial grimaces. Sometimes the warriors stick out their tongues.

◁ Hawaiian singers at a sacred festival beat on drums made from gourds, large dried and hollowed-out fruit or vegetable husks. Their songs are addressed to the gods and may be accompanied by a dance called the *hula*.

## TIME LINE

☞ **50,000BC** First peoples reach Australia

☞ **4000BC** The Pacific islands begin to be settled

☞ **AD1000** New Zealand is settled

☞ **1770** Captain James Cook charts coast of Australia

☞ **1778** Europeans build first settlement in Australia at Sydney Cove

♪ **1820s** Hawaiian music prohibited by missionaries

☞ **1828** Aborigines made to live on reservations

☞ **1967** Aborigines gain right to vote

☻ **1973** Sydney Opera House opens

☞ **1995** French nuclear tests in South Pacific

▽ The Pacific Ocean covers about a third of the world's surface. Oceania stretches from Hawaii to New Zealand. Australia lies to the west.

# Eastern Asia

The musical traditions of this region go back thousands of years. Much ancient Chinese music was written for court dances and musical theatre, while Japan's celebrated *No* plays are an elaborate mixture of theatre, music and dancing. However, instrumental music is no less important. Many solo pieces attempt to evoke particular poetic sensations in the listener, such as the haunting 'Autumn Moon in the Han Palace' from China, or 'The Distant Sound of the Deer' from Japan.

Music also plays a vital role in religious ceremonies. It has strong links with Shinto, the most ancient religion of Japan. In Thailand music is performed during Buddhist rites and rituals. Percussion instruments of all kinds – drums, gongs, cymbals and bells – are used to placate the gods or to scare away demons. Perhaps the most remarkable ceremonial music of all is made by the *gamelan* orchestras of Java and Bali. According to legend, the first *gamelan* was created by the ancient gods who spoke to one another by beating gongs and tinkling chimes.

△ A flute player performing at the Chinese court 500 years ago. Musicians played at festivals, banquets and on the emperor's birthday.

△ The Korean *p'i p'a* is an ancient plucked instrument that has been played for over 2,000 years. It is also popular in China.

◁ Japanese religious ceremonies often make use of large drums as well as gongs and high-pitched flutes. This enormous drum belongs to a Japanese Shinto temple. Followers of the Shinto religion worship the spirits of their ancestors.

▷ A Buddhist monk in a Tibetan monastery calls his fellow monks to prayer by striking a frame drum. Buddhists chant their prayers.

◁ The *gamelan* orchestras of Java and Bali contain a wide array of different percussion instruments. *Gamelans* are heard at all kinds of occasions, and provide accompaniment to the famous Balinese 'shadow plays'.

**TIME LINE**

✎ **c.2000BC** Chinese Yellow River civilisation begins

♪ **c.1000BC** First mouth organ used in China

✎ **50BC–AD50** Buddhism introduced into China

♪ **c.100** First *gamelan*-like instruments brought to Java from India

♪ **c.500** Gongs first used in China

♪ **700s** Japanese court music developed

♪ **1300s** *No* plays first performed in Japan

✎ **1368–1644** Ming emperors rule China

🎭 **c.1800** Peking Opera developed

✎ **1945** Atomic bomb dropped on Hiroshima in Japan

✎ **1949** Mao Tse-Tung creates Chinese People's Republic

▽ Eastern Asia consists of China, Korea, Japan, Thailand, Vietnam, Malaya and the many islands of Indonesia.

# India and its Neighbours

△ Dancers celebrate a wedding in this Indian painting dating back to the 1500s. Their graceful movements are accompanied by tambourines, drums and wind instruments.

The vast region of the Indian sub-continent is home to many different peoples. Hundreds of musical traditions exist side by side, each with their own songs, dances and instrumental music. Different instruments are favoured in different areas. Stringed instruments such as the *sitar* and the bowed fiddle are popular in northern India, while a variety of flutes and trumpets are favoured in the south.

The best known Indian classical music comes from the north. It is based on a complicated series of scales called *ragas*, each one particular to a special mood, time of day and season. To play this kind of music with its intricate patterns of notes and rhythms requires many years of practice.

The voice is also highly regarded as an instrument and this region has some of the richest song collections in the world. Most are religious songs inspired by the Hindu, Muslim and Buddhist faiths. The soaring, expressive melodies of Qawaali music, played in India and Pakistan, are thought to bring both the listener and the performer closer to god.

◁ On the banks of the river Ganges in India, a *tabla* player drums out the rhythm as a *sitar* player performs an intricate scale, or *raga*. There are over 200 different *ragas* in Indian classical music.

▷ Religious celebrations take place throughout the year in India and the surrounding countries. In Kandy, Sri Lanka, elephants accompanied by dancers and drummers lead a procession in the Kandy Esala Perahera. This ten-day long festival honours a sacred tooth that is believed to have once belonged to Buddha.

## TIME LINE

👁 **c.3000BC** Indus Valley civilization founded (now Pakistan)

👁 **c.563BC** Birth of Buddha

👺 **c.400BC** *Mahabharata*, the world's longest poem, is begun

👁 **273BC** Emperor Asoka rules India and spreads Buddhism

👁 **AD1000** Muslim invasion of India

♪ **1200s** Development of *ragas*

👁 **1757** Start of British control of India

👁 **1947** India and Pakistan become independent

👁 **1948** Sri Lanka wins independence from British

◁ A Hindu singer from Bangladesh performs a traditional love song. A mixture of Asian and Western instruments provides the background for the highly expressive words.

▽ As well as the country of India, the Indian subcontinent includes Pakistan in the north-west, Nepal in the north, Bangladesh in the east and the island of Sri Lanka in the far south.

▷ Many of the instruments and folk songs performed in Pakistan, a Muslim country, echo the musical traditions of the Middle East.

# Indian Classical Dance

Music and dancing have been an important part of Indian culture for thousands of years. Many of the dances have close links with the Hindu religion, and are inspired by its myths and legends. These include tender love stories as well as tales of epic battles between gods and demons.

Different styles of dance developed in the various regions of India. *Bharat Natya* emerged from the temples in the south. *Kathakali*, which is danced only by men, comes from Kerala in the south-west. *Kathak*, from the north, is similar to Muslim court dances, while *Manipuri* folk dances originate in the north-east.

◁ A carved statue of a painted temple dancer holding a stringed instrument. From ancient times the word *sangita* has meant both music and dancing.

▽ The tinkling sound from an anklet of tiny bells draws attention to the dancer's legs and feet. Most Indian dance is performed barefoot.

## BHARAT NATYA POSES

△ Rama grieving over the loss of Sita

◁ Sita, the beautiful and virtuous

△ Sita lighting her lamp

△ Ravana, the evil demon king

▽ Rama destroying the demon king, Ravana

△ Vishnu, the supreme god

◁ King Dasaratha, Rama's father

◁ Poses in the *Bharat Natya* dance drama tell the story of Rama and Sita, two of the gods of Hindu mythology who faced many perils together. Other gods and demons are also portrayed in this dance.

**Right hand represents Rama's bow**

Indian classical dancers are among the most graceful in the world. Their gestures and poses convey a wide range of emotions. The body is divided into major sections (*anga*) of the head, torso, arms and legs. Minor sections (*upanga*) include the angle of the nose and chin, and movements of the eyes.

**Jingles ring out as dancer moves**

**Left hand represents Rama's arrows**

**Pose represents Rama, the great hunter**

◁ A *Bharat Natya* dancer depicts the god Rama. She is showing Rama holding a bow in one hand and arrows in the other. This is the oldest type of Indian classical dance. *Bharat Natya* is a dance only performed by women.

**Ankle bells**

**Feet stamp out rhythm**

▽ Hand and finger positions, called *mudras*, are a very expressive part of Indian dance. *Bharat Natya* has more than 50 different hand and finger postions.

▽ Tying a garland of flowers

▽ A flower blossoming

▽ Pointing to the Moon

▽ Krishna playing the flute

▽ Stroking a cow

▽ A bee landing on a flower

23

# The Heart of Africa

South of the Sahara lies the vast area known as Central Africa, with its varied landscape of mountains, rivers, forests and deserts. This area, containing over forty countries and hundreds of different tribes, is the source of a remarkable number of musical traditions. Common to all are powerful rhythms, beaten out on drums of every type and size.

The training a tribal drummer has to undergo is every bit as demanding as that of a Western classical musician, and often begins at an early age. Other instruments – most made from natural materials – also feature prominently in traditional African music. These include zithers and fiddles fashioned from gourds, flutes made of wood, and trumpets carved from ivory and animal horn.

But it is song that lies at the heart of much African music. There are songs to celebrate weddings and births, songs to help deal with sickness and death, and songs to accompany work. Whatever the event – big or small – there is usually some kind of song to mark its passing.

△ Sculptures of court drummers from the West African country of Benin, which prospered during the 1600 and 1700s.

▽ War dances are just one of many dances performed by the Zulu people of South Africa. There is even a Zulu dance for making a complaint to the local chief or king!

▷ Drumming dominates the music of the Yoruba people from Nigeria. The lead drummer of this percussion group is playing on an *iyalu* ('mother of the drums') which 'talks' by imitating Yoruba speech.

◁ In Zaire, Central Africa, tribal gatherings and dances are always accompanied by the rhythms of the drums. Xylophones, too, are commonly played. Here a witch doctor prepares to lead a ritual dance.

**TIME LINE**

☞ **c.150,000BC** Some of the earliest humans (remains found in Tanzania)

♪ **c.30,000–15,000BC** First musical bows developed

🦋 **8500BC** Rock paintings made in Sahara, then rich grassland

☞ **AD1100** Age of Great Zimbabwe flourishing in southeast Africa

☞ **1300** Benin kingdom founded in West Africa

☞ **1502** The first African slaves are taken to the Americas

☞ **1990** Apartheid (segregation of blacks and whites) is formally abolished in South Africa

☞ **1994** Nelson Mandela becomes President of the South African Republic

## FOOT DRUMS

African 'foot drums' are often carved in human shapes, and are designed to stand on their own two carved feet. Many of these drums have a ritual importance and are used in religious ceremonies. The drum is also used to beat out messages imitating speech – a very good way of communicating in dense jungle or over great stretches of grassland or desert.

▽ The heart of Africa includes countries from Nigeria and the Sudan all the way south to the South African Republic.

25

# The Middle East

△ The musician in the centre of this ancient Sumerian mosaic is playing a lyre, one of the oldest types of instrument and an ancestor of the harp. The Sumerian civilization developed in the land now known as Iraq.

The history of the different lands and peoples that make up the Middle East stretches back over 5,000 years. It was here that the first great civilizations of Sumer, Assyria, Babylon and Egypt developed. Among their musical legacies were the early ancestors of the modern violin, oboe and trumpet.

The Middle East was also the birthplace of the Jewish, Christian and Muslim faiths. The Bible contains a lot of references to music in early Jewish worship, including the chanting of psalms which was later taken up by Christians. The music of the early Eastern Church developed into the chants and hymns sung in Greek and Russian Orthodox churches today.

After its founding in AD600s, the Muslim faith – or Islam – quickly spread throughout the Middle East, North Africa and even into Spain. Intricate rhythms and sound patterns are typical of Muslim music. Singers known as *muezzin* still bring the faithful to prayer five times a day with a call which requires great skill to sing.

▷ A woman of the wandering Tuareg tribe in North Africa's Sahara Desert coaxes a tune from a one-stringed fiddle. This ancient instrument is often used to accompany songs usually sung by men.

△ These Muslim mystics, called dervishes, worship Allah (God) by repeating a prayer and performing a whirling dance which takes them into an ecstatic trance. Many religions still include dance in their ceremonies.

▽ The *shofar*, a wind instrument made from a ram's horn, was used by the Hebrew people in ancient times and is mentioned in the Bible. It can still be heard in synagogues during religious ceremonies.

△ The influence of Muslim culture in medieval Spain survives in modern Spanish flamenco dance. The stamping of the dancer's feet, the clicking of castanets and the accompanying chanted song all originally came from North Africa.

▽ Middle Eastern countries include Iran, Iraq, Syria, Saudi Arabia, Israel and Egypt. North Africa covers Tunisia, Algeria and Morocco.

# Latin America

A series of great empires once thrived in Mexico, Central and South America. The Mayans and later the Toltecs, Incas and Aztecs made music an important part of their way of life. An Aztec musician who played a wrong note during a religious ceremony could be put to death! Rattles, scrapers, drums and wind instruments formed the basis of these peoples' music.

During the 1500s, Spanish and Portuguese settlers and soldiers conquered many of the lands in this region. Some of the older types of music blended with the Spanish and Portuguese songs and dances to create what is known as Latin American music. Its lively rhythm was also influenced by the music African slaves brought with them when they were sent to work on the plantations of the Caribbean. Today, Latin American dance rhythms such as the tango, rumba, bossa nova and samba are enjoyed all over the world.

△ A Toltec figure made of pottery beats a drum. The Toltecs were a warrior-like people who ruled in Central America from AD900 to 1100.

△ The gentle sound of the panpipes is heard in Bolivia, Peru, Ecuador and parts of Argentina and Chile. This ancient instrument, known locally as the *antaras* or *zampoñas*, has bamboo pipes.

▽ A hunter from the Amazon rainforest plays a one-stringed bow. Biting hold of one end, he uses his mouth and teeth to resonate the sound and to change pitch.

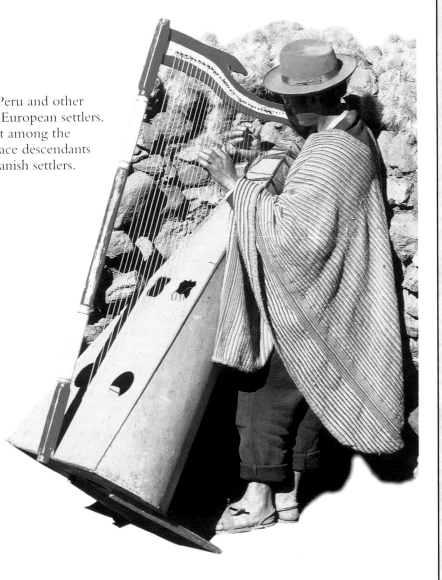

> The harp was introduced to Peru and other
parts of South America by early European settlers.
Today, it is a popular instrument among the
mestizos. These are the mixed-race descendants
of the native peoples and the Spanish settlers.

▽ The carnival of Rio de
Janeiro, Brazil, was originally
a religious festival. Today, it is
a riot of colour and high spirits
as thousands of dancers and
musicians throng the streets.

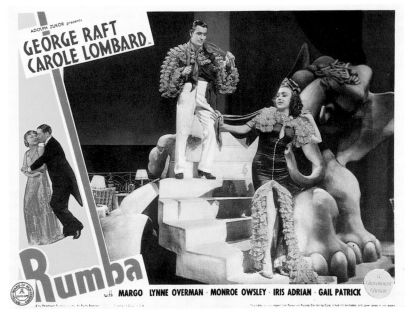

△ By the 1930s Latin American dances such as
the Cuban rumba were featuring in Hollywood
films. The energetic rhythms could also be heard
in dance halls and night clubs throughout Europe
and the United States. Later, the samba and the
conga became just as popular.

## TIME LINE

♪ **200–100BC** Flutes
and panpipes played
in the Andes

🎭 **c.AD250** Mayan
culture dominates
Central America

✍ **c.1300** Creation of
the Aztec empire in
Mexico and the Inca
empire in Peru

♀ **1492** Christopher
Columbus arrives in
the Caribbean islands

✍ **1521** Spanish
destroy Aztec empire

✍ **1532** Spanish
conquer Inca empire

✍ **1600s** Slaves
brought from Africa
to work in the
Caribbean

✍ **1824** Simon
Bolivar ends Spanish
rule in much of South
America

✍ **1959** Fidel Castro
becomes Communist
leader of Cuba

▽ Latin America
includes the whole
of South and Central
America and the
islands of the
Caribbean.

# Native Americans

The musical traditions of Native Americans go back thousands of years. Originally nomads, probably from Asia, these people settled in many parts of the Americas and over time developed their own distinctive customs.

Nevertheless, the music of the different tribes has much in common. Most of it is sung, either by a group or by a solo voice, and it reflects their belief in the spirits of the natural world.

Despite the loss of their land to Europeans, the native tribes of North America have preserved much of their music and dance. They still perform ancient ceremonial dances, including dances intended to bring rain or victory in battle. These are accompanied by chanting and drums.

△ A demon spirit painted on a drum head made of buffalo hide. The drum belonged to one of the tribes from the Great Plains in North America and was beaten to ward off evil spirits. Rattles, too, were used for this purpose.

▽ This Inuit Nootka rattle is shaped like a killer whale. The Nootkas live in and around Vancouver, Canada, and once hunted whales in dugout canoes.

▷ A Native American wearing ceremonial dress, including jingle bells round his legs. Many tribal dances imitate the behaviour of animals. The women of the Great Lakes tribes perform swaying dances, waving their arms to mime the flight of migrating wild swans and geese.

30

▷ These Native Americans are participating in a powwow, a festive gathering of tribes to celebrate their musical culture. This one takes place each year in Gallup, New Mexico.

▷ Inuit musicians beat vigorously on frame drums as they sing. They also make 'mouth music', adding grunts, hisses, snorts and whistles as they sing.

♀ **c.35,000BC** Native Americans first arrive from Asia

☞ **c.AD700** Mogollon, Anasazi and Hohokam, cultures flourishing in south-western North America

☞ **1830s** Many Native Americans are forced by US government to leave their lands and move west onto reservations

☞ **1861–65** American Civil War

♀ **1869** First trans-continental railroad completed

☞ **1876** Sioux Chief Sitting Bull defeats US troops at Battle of Little Big Horn

☞ **1886** Apache Chief Geronimo surrenders to US army

▽ Native North Americans include the Inuit, Iroquois, Sioux, Cherokee and Apache peoples. They live in an area that stretches from the Arctic Circle to Mexico.

# European Folk Music

Europe has a rich tradition of folk music. This is music which is a part of everyday life and is made by ordinary people. It is often accompanied by song and is passed down the generations by being listened to, rather than by being written down.

Every region in Europe – from the harsher northern lands to the sunnier southern countries – has its own folk music. Some instruments are typical of certain countries. The lute, for example, is common in Greece. It is hard to estimate the age of much folk music – one of its characteristics is that tunes and words may be reshaped with each performance, hiding the music's origin. Many of the folk songs we know today date back at least as far as the Middle Ages. Troubadours wandered all over Europe, picking up tales and legends, mixing folk ideas with courtly themes. Some folk songs deal with love, some are work songs, others celebrate the change in the seasons or important events. Many are for children. The music is often danced by groups in patterns of chains, lines and circles.

△ The Greek god Apollo plays his lyre. In ancient times poet-musicians such as Homer sung of epic battles and heroic deeds. Their words and melodies have been remembered and passed on in the folk music of various European countries.

△ The hurdy-gurdy dates from the 1100s. Musicians around that time sung at dances or rich peoples' feasts, accompanying themselves with instruments such as the rebec and the hurdy-gurdy.

▽ Russian Cossack dancers are well known for their high leaps and kicks. Many of them were originally peasant soldiers who fought for the Russian army.

◁ English Morris dancers
wear bells on their legs to
beat out the rhythms and
are usually accompanied by
an accordion. The Morris
dance was originally a
fertility ritual to encourage
spring rains to fall on crops.

◁ A French street
organist plays a
beautifully crafted
harmonium to passers-
by. A bellows causes
air to vibrate along
the reed pipes of
this keyboard
instrument.

## TIME LINE

☞ **c.490BC** Birth of
Pericles and golden
age of Greece

☞ **58–50BC** Julius
Caesar conquers Gaul
and lands in Britain

☞ **AD800**
Charlemagne
crowned Emperor of
the Holy Roman
Empire

☞ **1346** Black Death
enters Europe

☞ **1381** Peasants'
Revolt in England

✤ **1812** Grimm
Brothers' collection
of German folk tales
published

♪ **1902** Composer
Vaughan Williams
begins collection of
English folksongs

♪ **1905** Composer
Béla Bartók begins
collection of
Hungarian folksongs

☞ **1939–45** World
War II

☞ **1957** Treaty of
Rome, founding the
European Community

▽ Europe stretches
from the Ural
Mountains to the
Atlantic Ocean, and
from the North Cape
to the southern tip
of Spain.

# The Middle Ages

The Middle Ages span almost a thousand years of European history. They began with the break-up of the western Roman Empire in the AD470s and ended in the 1400s when some of the countries we know today were beginning to take shape. In the early Middle Ages, the Christian Church began to develop a type of music known as plainsong. Based on ancient Jewish chanting, this music was sung in unison and without any accompanying instruments.

In about AD1000 Guido d'Arezzo, a Benedictine monk, invented staff notation. This way of writing down music had a major impact on the way music was sung. Western music moved away from its Middle Eastern origins and developed harmony, which is writing two or more notes to be played together in the form of chords. In the mid-1300s Guillaume de Machaut was celebrated for the harmonies and beauty of his music. For the first time, composers were recognized as artists with their own individual styles.

△ In this illuminated manuscript from the 1070s, King David plucks a harp. Below him a minstrel plays a rebec, an early ancestor of the violin.

▽ *Summer is coming in*, an English song composed around 1310, celebrates the end of winter. The words are written in English and Latin.

△ Guido d'Arezzo, shown here on the left, invented staff notation. This way of writing down notes is still used today.

## WANDERING MUSICIANS

Outside the Church, a whole range of secular (non-religious) music was performed during the Middle Ages. From about AD1000 students known as Goliards began to wander from court to court across Europe reciting poetry and songs. Jongleurs were travelling performers who entertained audiences in towns and villages with musical performances, juggling and acrobatic feats. During the late 1100s and 1200s, poet-musicians called troubadours sang tales of courtly love and chivalry.

◁ In the Middle Ages, Christians believed that the end of the world would be heralded by angels blowing trumpets. This picture was painted in Germany during the 1400s.

# The Renaissance

Meaning literally 're-birth', the Renaissance was a time when art and learning were revived. It began in Italy in the late 1300s and over the next two centuries spread throughout Europe. Also at this time people began exploring the rest of the world and challenging accepted beliefs.

The music of the Renaissance had a new depth and richness. It often consisted of several melodic lines, or tunes, played or sung at the same time. This is called polyphony. Some splendid choral polyphonic music was written by composers from northern France and Flanders such as Guillaume Dufay and Josquin Desprez.

Religious music was deeply affected by the Protestant Reformation of the 1500s. Wishing to give the people a more active part in worship, the reformers provided simple hymns for them to sing. In response, the Roman Catholic Church provided new and easier-to-follow music for its worshippers.

Many developments took place in non-religious music. Gentlefolk enjoyed courtly dancing as well as playing and singing music for their own entertainment. A favourite form of song was the madrigal, which was arranged to be sung by several people. These songs, usually about love, capture the self-confidence of this new age.

IOANNIS PETRI
Loisij Praenestini in basilica
S. Petri de vrbe cappellae
Magistri
MISSARVM LIBER PRIMVS

△ In this title page illustration from a book of his Masses, an Italian composer, Palestrina, presents his works to Pope Julius III.

◁ The *lira da braccio*, an early relative of the violin, had five strings that were bowed, plus two that vibrated. It was often used to accompany poetry about fictitious heroes and gods.

▽ Thomas Tallis was one of the best-known composers in the reign of Queen Elizabeth I. He wrote a lot of music for the English Church, including a choral work with 40 separate parts *Spem in alium.*

△ Learning to read and perform music was part of the education of every aristocrat. In *The Concert*, painted by an anonymous artist in the early part of the 1500s, two ladies play a flute and a lute, while a third prepares to sing.

◁ The clavicytherium was an early, upright form of the harpsichord. This one was made in the late 1400s. As in a piano, the long strings produce low notes, the shorter strings higher notes. However, the strings are not struck but plucked by a quill attached to a wooden block, or jack. Like most early keyboard instruments, it is elaborately decorated.

# The Baroque Period

During the Baroque period (about 1600 to 1750), music became increasingly complex. Both instrumental and vocal music contained passages of many quick notes in rapid succession which required great skill to perform. Singers were expected to give excitement to slower melodies by adding their own notes.

Music became more dramatic, featuring contrasts between loud and soft, fast and slow, large groups of performers and small ones. Drama and passion found their perfect outlet in a brand-new musical form called opera. This developed from spectacular court entertainments in Italy in the early 1600s. Soon public opera houses were springing up all over Europe and leading opera singers became well-known celebrities.

One of Baroque's leading composers, Johann Sebastian Bach, wrote music for the harpsichord and organ. His fugues – complicated pieces of music – are like moving, three-dimensional puzzles.

△ Claudio Monteverdi was the first great composer of opera. He wrote religious music for groups of performers placed up in the church galleries to create a kind of heavenly dialogue.

▷ The Crook horn was a popula orchestral instrument throughou the 1700s. By attaching different coiled tubes the player could produce tones in different keys.

◁ During the Baroque era composers such as Johann Sebastian Bach and George Frideric Handel wrote major pieces for the organ. This 'King of instruments' was often housed in churches that were extravagantly and elaborately decorated – reflecting much of the music of the period.

◁ Johann Sebastian Bach is shown here at the keyboard, surrounded by some of his many children and his second wife, Anna Magdalena (standing centre). Several of Bach's sons became important composers.

▽ George Frideric Handel was best known as a composer of operas and oratorios. His most famous oratorio is the *The Messiah*. Handel also produced a great deal of music for the orchestra, including the *Water Music*.

**TIME LINE**

♪ **1607** First performance of Monteverdi's opera *Orfeo* in Mantua, Italy

☜ **1642–48** English Civil War

♀ **1687** Sir Isaac Newton's theory of gravity published

♪ **c.1700** The piano is invented

☜ **1703** Tsar Peter the Great of Russia begins building St. Petersburg

♣ **1719** Ancient city of Pompeii discovered in Italy

♪ **1729** First performance of Bach's *St Matthew Passion*

♪ **1742** First performance of Handel's *The Messiah* in Dublin

♣ **1755** Samuel Johnson's dictionary of the English language published

# The Classical Age

△ This plaque made in the late 1700s shows Homer playing the lyre. In this period Greek art was much admired. Classical composers aimed for an equally harmonious effect in their music.

▽ Music was a vital part of court life, especially at the court of Frederick the Great of Prussia. As well as composing music, he was an accomplished player of the flute.

Around the mid–1700s, the Baroque style began to seem old-fashioned. People now preferred music that was more restrained and balanced. These qualities were characteristic of the art of ancient Greece and Rome, the 'classical' civilizations, which gave this period which lasted into the 1820s, its name. However, some of the musical forms from the Baroque period remained popular, evolving to suit the new taste and improved instruments. Among them was the solo concerto, a piece of music written for an orchestra but featuring a specific instrument. Mozart wrote 21 piano concertos.

New forms, too, were created. The symphony, a work for the orchestra, usually in four contrasting movements, was developed, and perfected by Franz Joseph Haydn. Like the concerto it attracted large audiences to public concerts, now an important part of the musical scene. The string quartet and other pieces written for small groups also became very popular.

◁ Franz Joseph Haydn's opera *L'incontro Improvviso* (The Unexpected Encounter) was first performed at the palace of the Esterházy family, Hungary. The conductor, seated at the keyboard as was the custom, may be Haydn himself.

▷ Wolfgang Amadeus Mozart was a brilliant keyboard player as well as a composer. Here, he is seen with his sister and his father Leopold.

◁ In this scene from the 1818 Munich production of Mozart's opera *The Magic Flute*, designed by Simon Quaglio, the Queen of the Night makes a dramatic entrance. This opera contains some of the loveliest music Mozart ever wrote – produced at a time (1791) when he was racked with debt and illness.

♪ **1754** First performance of Mozart's opera *Don Giovanni,* in Prague

☻ **1759** Publication of Voltaire's satirical novel *Candide*

☞ **1775-83** American War of Independence

☞ **1789** Storming the Bastille in Paris launches the French Revolution

♪ **1791–92** Haydn's first visit to London

♀ **1799** Metric system of measurement introduced in France

☻ **1813** Publication of Jane Austen's novel *Pride and Prejudice*

☞ **1815** Napoleon Bonaparte defeated at the Battle of Waterloo

♪ **1824** First performance of Beethoven's *Symphony No. 9,* in Vienna

# Beethoven

▽ A death mask of
Beethoven. Such
masks, modelled
directly on the dead
person's face, were
used to commemorate
famous people.

The world into which Ludwig van
Beethoven was born, in 1770, was on the
brink of great changes. When he was five
the American Colonies declared their
independence from Britain; when he
was 22 years old, the French king
was guillotined by revolutionaries.
There was a new interest in heroic
figures as reflected in the poems
of Byron. It is not surprising
that *Fidelio,* the one
opera Beethoven
wrote, is about
heroism and the
fight for freedom.

▷ *Napoleon Crossing the Alps*, by Jacques Louis David,
shows the General in heroic form, intent on conquest.
Napoleon Bonaparte came to power in France as a leader
of the revolution against foreign enemies, then went on
to bring other parts of Europe under French rule.

▷ Beethoven
originally dedicated
his third symphony,
the *Eroica*, to
Napoleon Bonaparte,
whom he greatly
admired. But when he
learned that his hero
had made himself
emperor, Beethoven
scratched out the
original dedication
and wrote 'Heroic
Symphony, composed
to celebrate the
memory of a great
man.'

n Beethoven's music we find a change taking place from the elegant
tyle typical of the 1700s to the more dramatic, personal approach that
would dominate the next century. Some of his early piano sonatas,
for instance, contain music of great tenderness, but there are also
turbulent passages, such as the first movement of the *Pathétique*
sonata (1799), a hint of things to
come. In later works,
he developed ideas
in greater depth,
producing very
intense and
fiery music.

▽ This portrait of Beethoven,
at work on his *Missa Solemnis*
('Solemn Mass'), was painted by
Joseph Carl Steiler when the
composer was 49. It shows
him as handsome
and soulful. He
died in 1827,
aged 56.

△ Some
of the ear
trumpets that
Beethoven used after
he realised, in the late
1790s, that he was
going deaf. Although
he could still hear
music in his head well
enough to compose,
he could no longer
play or conduct.

43

# The Romantic Spirit

△ These musical kittens, scrambling over the staves, are generally believed to have been drawn by Schubert. But the artist was probably one of the composer's friends, Moritz von Schwind.

In the early 1800s, the arts focused on themes that we call 'romantic', such as the beauty of nature, the power of the imagination and the supernatural. There was also a new interest in the art and music of the Middle Ages. These themes were explored by composers such as Franz Liszt and Hector Berlioz.

Liszt invented a new single-movement musical form, called the symphonic poem. He used this to convey dramatic themes or stories. Franz Schubert wrote hundreds of songs both as settings for Romantic poems and to express his feelings of longing and sadness. Other composers used the symphony to 'paint' spectacular landscapes in sound or to evoke dreams and emotions. Berlioz's *Symphonie Fantastique,* for example, describes in part 'fantastic' scenes from his own vivid imagination.

△ The dazzling technique of the violinist Nicolò Paganini (1782–1840), and his strange, dark features, led to claims that he was possessed by the devil.

◁ Unlike classical concertos, in which solo and orchestra were well-balanced, those by Franz Liszt were mainly a showcase for the soloist. This cartoon shows Liszt, with keyboard wings, delivering a mortal blow to the orchestra's 'General Bass'.

▷ The upper scenes of *The Symphony*, by Moritz Schwind, suggest different themes for a composition. In the bottom scene the finished work is being performed. Franz Schubert can be seen standing in the background, third from left.

◁ Frédéric Chopin (seen here in a photograph taken in the 1840s) was one of the greatest pianists of the age although he only performed in public 30 times. Most of his compositions are for piano, and many are based on the folk dances of his native Poland.

# Late Romanticism

In the late 1800s symphonies became longer and required even larger orchestras. Gustav Mahler's *Symphony No. 3* requires a huge orchestra, two choirs and a solo singer. It has six movements and lasts about ninety minutes. Music also continued to be used as a way of expressing emotion. A powerful example is Pyotr Ilyich Tchaikovsky's *Symphony No. 6*, which has been called a 'symphonic suicide note'.

The work of other composers, such as Modest Mussorgsky, Nicolai Rimsky-Korsakov, Antonin Dvořák and Edvard Grieg illustrate a new trend – nationalism. This kind of music often included folk elements to help express patriotism. The operas of Richard Wagner drew their stories mainly from Germanic legend, but the music was startlingly original. Traditionally, opera had comprised songs (arias and choruses), linked by recitative (a kind of sung speech). Wagner replaced this structure with a continuous flow of music containing short melodic pieces called *leitmotifs*. Each *leitmotif* represented a character, place, object, idea or feeling. Giuseppe Verdi's operas contained more traditional harmonies. His glorious melodies, driving rhythms and dramatic stories brought Italian opera to a new peak.

△ Richard Wagner's *Ring*, a cycle made up of four operas, was his crowning achievement. Over some 18 hours (with intervals), it tells a story of love, heroism, greed and treachery. This is a scene from the last opera, *The Twilight of the Gods*.

▽ Johannes Brahms' music combines romanticism with a preference for classical structure. He also loved folk music. Shown here is one of his *Hungarian Dances*.

△ Gustav Mahler was better known in his day as a conductor than as a composer. He occupied several important posts, including that of conductor of the Vienna Opera. Here a cartoonist shows him (left) conducting in Paris.

△ The lighter side of Viennese music was captured in the dances of Johann Strauss the Younger. This cartoon, drawn after his death, shows him in heaven conducting one of his waltzes. Around him dance the ghosts of other composers, including his friend Brahms (third from right), Bach, Mozart and Beethoven.

▷ A scene from
Giuseppe Verdi's *Nabucco*
(Nebuchadnezzar), which is
about the Hebrews' captivity in
Babylon. Verdi's patriotism – he
was a fervent supporter of the
unification of Italy – can be
heard in this opera's stirring
choruses, as well as in some of
his other operas.

## TIME LINE

☎ **1861–65** American Civil War

📖 **1869** Leo Tolstoy's novel *War and Peace* published

☎ **1870** Unification of Italy completed

🎭 **1869** First exhibition of Impressionist painting, in Paris

♪ **1871** First performance of Verdi's opera *Aida*

♪ **1871** First performance of Wagner's *Ring,* in Bayreuth, Germany

💡 **1877** Thomas Edison invents the phonograph (wax cylinder-type model)

☎ **1883** Eruption of Mount Krakatoa, in Indonesia, killing 36,000 people

💡 **1895** X-rays discovered by Wilhelm Roentgen

♪ **1899** First performance of Sir Edward Elgar's *'Enigma' Variations*, in Birmingham, England

# Music of the Modern Age

The music of our own century has undergone many changes. In the early 1900s, Debussy was using sounds to suggest images in a similar way to Impressionist painting. Although his harmonies were new, they presented no great challenge to audiences. The real shock came with Igor Stravinsky's ballet *The Rite of Spring*. With its violent, hammering rhythms it caused a riot at its Paris première.

At the same time, Arnold Schoenberg was developing his 12-tone system, in which the sense of key was eliminated. Other composers later adopted this system, including Karlheinz Stockhausen.

A later development was random music, in which the sounds produced are decided either by the performers (who are given only guidelines) or by chance. The main figure in this movement was John Cage. He used all sorts of sounds, from radio static to fragments of speech in his pieces.

Minimalism, which emerged in the early 1960s, is the repetition or gradual variation of a short theme over a long period. Leading minimalist composers include Philip Glass, Steve Reich and Arvo Pärt.

△ Claude Debussy's *Prelude à l'Après-midi d'un Faune* was made into a ballet in which the leading role was taken by the famous dancer Vaslav Nijinsky. This picture is by Leon Bakst, the ballet's designer.

▷ Igor Stravinsky, shown here at work, is arguably the most important composer of the century. Over a period of nearly 60 years he drew on influences many from classical to jazz music.

∇ The music of Karlheinz Stockhausen relies heavily on electronics. In an early piece, *Song of the Youths*, he recorded a chorister singing a psalm. He then transformed the boy's voice in various ways and combined it with snatches of electronically produced sounds. Inventions such as the synthesizer and computer have vastly expanded the range of sounds available to composers.

▷ *The Cave,* by minimalist composer Steve Reich, is a multi-media work based on the Biblical figure, Abraham. As well as a traditional chamber orchestra and four singers, the piece makes use of the latest video technology. The words and pictures that accompany the music are projected onto five large screens.

◁ The sounds for some modern music require completely new kinds of notation. These coloured marks are for György Ligeti's electronic piece *Artikulations*.

💡 **1903** Wright brothers make first flight in a powered aircraft

🎭 **1907** First cubist painting, Pablo Picasso's *Les Demoiselles d'Avignon*

🎭 **1927** First talking film, *The Jazz Singer* released

♪ **1935** First performance of George Gershwin's opera, *Porgy and Bess*

☞ **1939–45** World War II

♪ **1945** First performance of Benjamin Britten's opera, *Peter Grimes*

♪ **1954** Start of rock and roll

👁 **1963** Assassination of US President John F. Kennedy

🎭 **1973** Sydney Opera House finished

💡 **1990** Hubble Space Telescope launched by US

# *Jazz*

King Oliver's Dixie Syncopators
Plantation Cafe
Chicago Ill

Jazz was born in the 1890s in the southern city of New Orleans, USA. African-Americans combined the energy and rhythms of African music with the sounds and instruments of the West. It was the beginning of a totally new style of music. Condemned at first as 'the Devil's music', jazz nevertheless soon spread across the USA and later the world. Its power to dazzle audiences has long been associated with brilliant instrumentalists such as the brass player Louis Armstrong and the pianist Duke Ellington. But along with the famous players, women singers such as Bessie Smith and Billie Holiday also emerged as important musicians.

In the 1930s dance band leaders Benny Goodman and Glenn Miller brought a new style of jazz called 'swing' to a much wider audience. After World War II, increasingly complex music was developed by pioneers like Charlie Parker and Miles Davis. Today, all jazz styles – from traditional New Orleans to the most recent fusion between jazz and rock – remain popular.

△ Top New Orleans jazzman Joe 'King' Oliver moved north to Chicago in 1920. With rising star Louis Armstrong playing cornet alongside him, Oliver's classic 1923 recordings helped the spread of jazz throughout the USA.

▷ Bessie Smith was one of the earliest jazz singers. Known as the 'Empress of the Blues' she sang in the blues scale. Unique to jazz and blues, this scale has a mournful and expressive sound.

△ In the late 1930s trombonist Glenn Miller led the top 'swing' band in the USA. Hits such as 'In the Mood' brought jazz to a wider and younger audience. Miller's performances, however, were brought to a sudden end in 1944, when his aircraft disappeared over the English Channel.

▷ An inspiring pianist, Thelonious Monk helped Charlie Parker and others create 'bebop'. Often fast and furious, the new jazz shocked more traditional fans. Monk's 'Round Midnight' is one of the most recorded jazz tunes of all time.

◁ The blistering cornet solos of Louis 'Satchmo' Armstrong took the jazz world by storm in the 1920s. Armstrong's mastery over the trumpet was equally superb, and singing in his distinctive growl, he went on to become a worldwide star.

▷ The brilliant technique of Wynton Marsalis has made him one of the most acclaimed jazz musicians playing today. He is equally at home playing the trumpet in classical music.

**TIME LINE**

☞ **1863** Slavery abolished in US

♪ **1890s** Development of ragtime

♪ **1903** Bessie Smith makes singing debut aged nine

☞ **1914** Outbreak of World War I

♪ **1920s** King Oliver and Jelly Roll Morton develop New Orleans jazz in Chicago and New York

🎭 **1927** *The Jazz Singer* released in US cinemas

☞ **1939** Outbreak of World War II

♪ **1940s** Start of the 'bebop' revolution

♪ **1955** Miles Davis stars at Newport Jazz Festival

♪ **1960s** Development of avant-garde 'free' jazz

☞ **1963** Assassination of President Kennedy

♪ **1970s** Early jazz–rock fusion experiments

♪ **1991** Death of Miles Davis

# Musicals

△ Irving Berlin made jazz an important part of musicals. He wrote the music and lyrics for a string of hits – even though he never learned how to read or write music.

The musical is a marriage of operetta, or light opera, and the British and American music-hall acts of the 1890s. The American composer Irving Berlin added one other vital ingredient – jazz. Early musicals had very thin storylines and the songs were little more than decoration. This all changed in the late 1920s with Jerome Kern's groundbreaking shows, especially *Show Boat*, which made the songs central to the story and covered more serious subjects.

The 1930s saw the sophisticated music and lyrics of Cole Porter, George and Ira Gershwin, Richard Rogers and Lorenz Hart become popular. But it was Rodgers' and Hammerstein's *Oklahoma!* which, in 1943, ushered in the golden age of the Broadway musical. Stephen Sondheim, a pupil of Hammerstein's, emerged as a brilliant composer in the late 1950s. More recently rock music has made its influence felt, and in the 1970s and 1980s British shows, especially those of Andrew Lloyd Webber, began to dominate the world of musicals.

▽ *Show Boat*, first performed in 1927, was Jerome Kern's masterpiece. It was one of the first musicals in which the songs, such as 'Ol' Man River', are central to the story.

▷ *Oklahoma!*, opened in 1943 and began 30 years of world-wide dominance for the Broadway musical. It boasted a ballet, superb songs and a dramatic storyline. It was songwriter Oscar Hammerstein II's and composer Richard Rodgers' first show together.

△ For over 70 years New York's Broadway has been the home of American musicals. Today shows from England, such as *Les Misérables*, also enjoy great critical and public acclaim.

◁ *Singin' in the Rain*, which appeared in 1952, is considered one of the greatest screen musicals. The film, starring Gene Kelly, makes fun of the early days of the 'talkies' (films with recorded sound).

△ Packed with romance and mystery *The Phantom of the Opera* is one of Andrew Lloyd Webber's most spectacular shows. Other smash hits include *Starlight Express* and *Cats*.

## TIME LINE

♪ **1858** First full-scale operetta – *Orpheus in the Underworld*

🎭 **1895** First public screening of a film, in Paris

💡 **1906** First radio programme broadcast in America

☞ **1914** Outbreak of World War I

♪ **1927** First performance of *Show Boat*

☞ **1929** Wall Street stock market crash

☞ **1939** World War II begins

♪ **1943** Richard Rodgers writes *Oklahoma!* with Oscar Hammerstein II

🎭 **1952** *Singin' in the Rain* released

♪ **1957** Stephen Sondheim makes Broadway debut as lyricist for *West Side Story*

♪ **1968** *Hair*, the first rock musical, opens

♪ **1986** *Phantom of the Opera* opens in London

♪ **1996** Andrew Lloyd Webber's *Cats* becomes longest running musical in history of Broadway and London

# *West Side Story*

In 1957 *West Side Story* brought musical theatre up to date with a bang. The show took Shakespeare's classic love story *Romeo and Juliet* and moved it to the violent streets of New York. Director and choreographer Jerome Robbins came up with the original concept, but like all great musicals the end product was the result of successful teamwork. The combined talents of writer Arthur Laurents, composer Leonard Bernstein, lyricist Stephen Sondheim and Robbins himself proved to be a winning formula.

△ Leonard Bernstein (right) already had a successful career as a conductor and composer behind him, when he teamed up with newcomer Stephen Sondheim (left) to write the music for *West Side Story*.

Four years after its Broadway opening *West Side Story* was made into a brilliant film which went on to win two Academy Awards. With its depiction of prejudice, passion and gang warfare, both the screen version and stage show remain as powerful as ever for today's audiences.

△ Great musicals do not always make great films. *West Side Story* is one that did. The 1961 movie was a worldwide hit.

## ROMEO AND JULIET

First performed in 1596, *Romeo and Juliet* has always been one of Shakespeare's most popular plays. It tells the story of two young lovers from Verona, Italy, caught up in a bitter feud between their families, the Montagues and the Capulets. After Romeo and Juliet are secretly married, Romeo is exiled from Verona for killing a Capulet. The play ends with the two lovers taking their own lives. As well as *West Side Story*, this tragic story has inspired six operas, Tchaikovsky's *Romeo and Juliet Fantasy Overture* and a ballet by Prokofiev. There have also been many films of the play including seven silent versions as well as Franco Zeffirelli's famous 1968 film.

The writer Arthur Laurents turned Shakespeare's feuding Montagues and Capulets into rival gangs, the Jets and the Sharks. Ex-Jet Tony falls in love with Maria, sister of the Sharks' leader Bernardo. In a gang fight Bernardo kills Riff, the Jets' leader, with a knife. Tony then stabs Bernardo to death. *West Side Story* ends tragically, as Tony himself dies of gunshot wounds in Maria's arms.

▽ Jerome Robbins mixed ballet, jive and Latin American dance to create the thrilling movement that fills *West Side Story*. With Robert Wise he also co-directed the 1961 film version.

▽ To create real tension between the gangs, director Jerome Robbins encouraged the actors to stay in character both off-stage and on.

# Rock and Pop

∇ Elvis Presley burst onto the American pop scene in the 1950s. Singing raw rock and roll and swivelling his hips, he delighted his young fans.

The term 'popular music' can apply to anything from music-hall ballads to salsa. 'Pop' is a little more specific and includes everything from 1950s rock and roll to 1990s rap. Rock and roll was the first music to speak directly to young people. It mixed African-American rhythm and blues with white American country music. Elvis Presley made rock and roll a worldwide phenomenon. In Britain, the Beatles added their top-selling songwriting skills to rock and roll, while the Rolling Stones imitated the blues of Chicago. The Stones' loud, tough sound paved the way for the aggressive style of heavy metal. Meanwhile, Americans such as Aretha Franklin created a new blend of rhythm and blues and gospel music which came to be known as 'soul'. Disco music, which made heavy use of synthesizers, and rap music, are direct descendants of soul. In the late 1970s a new generation produced its own wild version of rock and roll called punk rock. The 1980s and 1990s saw new superstars, like Michael Jackson and Madonna, and groups such as U2, filling huge stadiums.

∇ In 1964 the Beatles returned home to a hero's welcome. Their first tour of the US launched an 'invasion' of British groups which inspired American bands.

▷ Johnny Rotten and his punk band, the Sex Pistols, played rock and roll at a frenzied speed using crude lyrics and rude gestures.

**TIME LINE**

♪ **1956** Elvis Presley's first US hit *Heartbreak Hotel*.

♪ **1960** Tamla Motown label founded in Detroit

☞ **1961** Berlin Wall built

♪ **1962** Beatles' first UK hit *Love Me Do*

♀ **1969** First landing on the Moon

♀ **1975** First video game launched in Japan

♪ **1982** First CDs go on sale

♪ **1985** Madonna has first number one *Like A Virgin*

☞ **1989** Berlin Wall knocked down

△ Tina Turner's career spans several decades of pop music. She had her first hits in the 1960s with her then husband, Ike Turner. Her solo career took off in the 1980s with the million-selling album *Private Dancer*.

▷ Since the late 1970s Bruce Springsteen has been one of the leading singer-guitarists, following the tradition of Eric Clapton. A sensational live performer, Springsteen also developed great skill as a songwriter.

57

# Introduction – Part One

△ Members of the chordophone, or string, family shown in a book published in 1618.

There are thousands of different instruments around the world. The variety of forms of the simple flute, for example, is almost endless. There are also many different methods of producing sound from instruments, and this is one way of classifying them. The ancient Greeks divided their instruments into two groups, those that were blown and those that were struck.

Today, one well-known classification is that of the Western orchestra, in which instruments are arranged into families of strings, woodwind, brass and percussion. Within these families instruments are further sub-divided by the way they are played. Another popular system also divides instruments up according to the way they produce sound. This system classifies instruments into five broad groups – idiophones, membranophones, chordophones, aerophones and electrophones.

## IDIOPHONES AND MEMBRANOPHONES

Examples of idiophones include the triangle, castanets, cymbals, woodblocks and the xylophone. In all these instruments sound is produced by the material from which the instrument itself is made. A membranophone produces sound by making a stretched skin vibrate. Most drums are membranophones. The common name for idiophones and membranophones is percussion instruments. Together these two groups make up the first section of this chapter.

The stretched skin of a drum vibrates when it is hit. The pitch of a drumhead can be altered by tightening or loosening the vibrating skin. If the skin is made less tight then the pitch of the note it makes will be lower. If the skin is tightened, the pitch of the note played will be higher. The smaller the drum the higher the sound will be because the area of the vibrating skin is reduced.

## CHORDOPHONES

In all chordophones, sound is produced by a string or strings stretched between two fixed points. Some of the most well-known examples are the violin, cello, harp and guitar. The pitch of a string depends upon its length, thickness and how tightly it is stretched. A short string will sound a higher pitch than a longer string. A thin string will sound a higher pitch than a thicker string. A tight string will sound a higher pitch than a looser string. Traditionally, strings were made from animal gut, hair, metal and, in Asia, silk. Today, they are usually made from nylon which lasts longer and is less easy to break. Chordophones are more often known as stringed instruments. This group makes up the second section of this chapter.

◁ On instruments such as the violin, or guitar, players sound different pitches on the same string by 'stopping' the string. Pressing the string against the fingerboard alters the vibrating length of the string and changes the pitch.

## INSTRUMENTS

△ The violin is played with a bow made of horsehair. This is covered with rosin to make the bow 'grip' the strings.

△ Plucking strings with fingers or a piece of hard material called a plectrum, produces different sounds.

△ Dulcimers are played with two wooden beaters or padded sticks which are held by the musician. Beaters can be straight or curved.

△ The sound of a vibrating string will be weak unless the string is attached to a resonator. This makes the vibrations louder. The violin's resonator is the hollow body, called a soundbox.

## BANGING AND CRASHING

Some drums are played with the hands. All parts of the hands can be used, including the fingers, the knuckles and the palm, to produce a range of different sounds.

The crash of the cymbals is one of the most exciting of all instrumental sounds. The player stops the vibrations of the cymbals by pressing them against his or her clothing.

Some drums are played with beaters. These can range from a pair of hard wooden sticks to sticks with a pad of soft felt at the tip. A blow with a hard stick produces a more explosive sound than a blow with a padded stick. Drums can also be played with brushes which produce a softer sound.

# Introduction – Part Two

△ A drawing of early
wind instruments, or
aerophones, made in
the early 1600s.

## AEROPHONES

Wind instruments of all kinds are classed as
aerophones. These are tubelike instruments
that produce sound when the air blown
into them vibrates. Two major groups of
instruments are aerophones – woodwind
(including flute, clarinet and oboe) and
brass (including trumpet, trombone and
French horn). Woodwind have holes in
them, which may be covered by 'keys'. Most
brass instruments have valves on them (right).
Both affect the pitch of sound produced.
When a hole is stopped on a flute, or a
valve pressed down on a trumpet, the air
inside the instrument is 'lengthened'.
This produces a low note.

△ Pressed down, the piston
valve forces air through extra
tubing – the note is deepened.

△ Rotary valves also force air
through extra tubing, but are
only used on French horns.

◁ The metal mouthpiece of a tuba (top) and a
trumpet (bottom). When the player blows down
the mouthpiece of a brass instrument, it vibrates.
Vibration of air is greatest at the mouthpiece and
at the flared end of the instrument's tube, the 'bell'.

▷ Mouthpieces of
various woodwind
instruments. From left
to right – oboe, flute,
recorder and clarinet.
The oboe and clarinet
have reeds – thin
strips of cane in the
mouthpiece vibrate
when blown. The
recorder is a member
of the flute family.

## HOW KEYBOARDS WORK

The harpsichord is a plucked string instrument. When the player presses a key (below), a 'jack' moves up and plucks the string.

When a piano key is pressed down (below), a system of levers causes a hammer to strike a tuned string. When the key is released, a 'damper' stops further vibrations of the string.

## ELECTROPHONES

Electrophones are musical instruments such as the electric guitar and synthesizer in which sounds are either picked up and amplified, or electronically generated. The synthesizer (above) can be played like a piano, while controls above the keyboard transform the notes into original and often strange sounds. The synthesizer also has a huge computer memory which can play back stored sounds while the musician improvises over them. Although the electric guitar is the best known example in which air vibrations are converted into an electric signal, this principle can also be applied to almost any acoustic instrument. There have been experiments with violins, double basses, clarinets, flutes, saxophones – and many others.

## KEYBOARD INSTRUMENTS

Keyboard instruments are difficult to classify. The organ is strictly an aerophone, and the harpsichord and piano are strictly chordophones. The link between all these instruments is that the player presses down a key to operate a mechanism that produced the sound. The keys on a piano cause small hammers to strike tuned strings. On a harpsichord, the keys control a mechanism that plucks the strings. Pressing a key on an organ opens a pipe in which a column of air vibrates. Some of the pipes can also be operated by foot pedals.

△ An electric guitar has no need of a resonator, or sound box, as an acoustic guitar does. Instead, an electronic 'pick up' converts the vibrations from its strings into electric signals. These signals are passed through an amplifier, which makes them much more powerful. Loudspeakers then convert the signals into sound.

# The Human Voice

The human voice is the most natural musical instrument of all. It is also one of the most expressive, whether it belongs to a folk singer or to a highly trained opera star. All singing is a complex process. Sound is produced when air from the lungs is forced past the vocal cords. Notes of different pitch are made according to how quickly or slowly these cords vibrate. Singers give expression to sound when they learn how to control their breathing and the muscles around the mouth.

All around the world people enjoy the sound of the human voice and there are endless ways of using it in a musical setting. Traditions of story-telling set to music are still very strong in China and other Far Eastern countries. In Islamic countries, the voice of a *muezzin*, or crier, summons people to prayer several times every day. And in Australia, singing forms a vital part of the Aborigine people's culture as a means of celebrating and passing on their history and beliefs.

△ Angels are said to have the purest voices of all. This sculpture from the 1400s depicts them in mid-song.

▽ The vocal cords are tightened when someone speaks or sings. Breathing out makes the cords vibrate and produce sound.

Low note –
vocal cords relaxed

High note – vocal cords taut

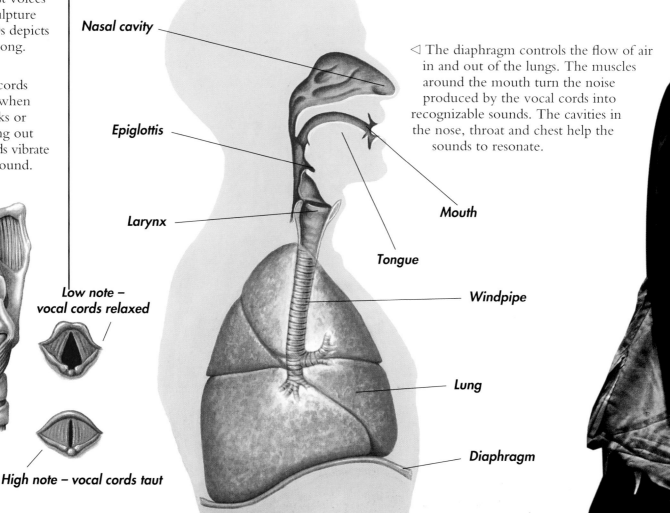

Nasal cavity

Epiglottis

Larynx

◁ The diaphragm controls the flow of air in and out of the lungs. The muscles around the mouth turn the noise produced by the vocal cords into recognizable sounds. The cavities in the nose, throat and chest help the sounds to resonate.

Mouth

Tongue

Windpipe

Lung

Diaphragm

## VOCAL RANGE

The natural pitch range of the human voice depends upon the shape and size of the throat and mouth. Men have deeper voices than women because they generally have larger larynxes with longer vocal cords. Women's voices fall into three ranges – soprano, mezzo-soprano and contralto (in descending order of pitch). The tenor, baritone and bass are the male equivalents.

Soprano

Tenor

Mezzo-soprano

Baritone

Contralto

Bass

◁ In many operas, the tenor voice is used to sing the part of the hero, the soprano voice that of the heroine and the bass voice that of the villain.

△ The technique of singing into a microphone is quite different from opera singing. Opera singers have to 'throw', or project, their voices so that people some distance away can hear them. Singers who use microphones have their voices projected electronically.

△ Boy sopranos, or trebles, have sung in European church and cathedral choirs since the Middle Ages. This practice dates from times when women were forbidden to sing in church. Today, however, some services are also sung by girls' choirs.

### LISTEN FOR

**BOY'S TREBLE**
Geoffrey Burgon –
*Nunc Dimittis*

**CHORAL WORKS**
George Handel –
*Messiah*

Wolfgang Amadeus Mozart –
*Requiem*

**OPERAS**
Gioachino Rossini –
*The Barber of Seville*

Giacomo Puccini –
*Madam Butterfly*

**WORLD MUSIC**
Songs by Salif Keita,
Miriam Makeba and
Youssou N'Dour

**LATIN AMERICAN MUSIC**
Songs by Celia Cruz,
Joe Arroyo, Joao Gilberto

# *Drums*

From the earliest times drums have been associated with magic and ritual, pounded in battles and parades or used to send messages over long distances. A drum beat provides the pulse that drives the music forwards in a Native American ceremonial dance or an explosive rock and roll song. In Western orchestras drums often bring a symphony to a dramatic and thunderous climax.

Many drums have a skin stretched tightly across a frame. When the skin is struck by a beater or a hand, its vibrations give out the sound. Some instruments such as the kettledrums, or timpani, have to be carefully tuned to the correct pitch. Others, such as the Japanese *tsuzumi*, have to be struck with exactly the right force. And a good sense of rhythm is always vital.

△ A frame drum beats out the rhythm for this Native American Buffalo dance, which was painted in the 1800s. Most frame drums are made of thin wood and skin and are light enough to be held in one hand.

▷ A modern Western orchestra usually has two or three kettledrums, or timpani. The timpanist can change the pitch of the instrument by moving the foot pedal up and down. The pedal is attached to tension rods which tighten or loosen the drum head.

**Drum sticks have padded ends**

**Tension rod**

**Tuning gauge indicates pitch of drum head**

**Foot pedal changes pitch of drum**

△ The Indian *tabla* is made up of two drums, each tuned to a different pitch. The player strikes the drum heads with the fingers of both hands.

## PERCUSSION

In a Western orchestra all the percussion instruments are located at the rear. They include timpani, a gong, a xylophone, a side drum and a bass drum.

▷ The *tsuzumi*, from Japan, is a small hand-held drum. A silk cord secures the skins at either end. The player can change the pitch of the drum by squeezing the cord to tighten the skin.

**Drum head made of plastic or calfskin**

**Connecting mechanism links tension rod with drum head**

**Supporting strut**

**Bowl made of copper**

**Wheel makes drum easier to move**

▽ The twirling drum is a small drum on a stick. When the drum is spun around, two balls rattle against the drum head.

▽ British musician Evelyn Glennie (born 1965) is famous for her solo performances on a wide range of percussion instruments. She is deaf, but feels the vibrations of the music through her sense of touch.

## ATTACHING THE DRUM HEAD

In some drums the stretched skin, or drum head, is laced to a second skin at the other end of the frame.

In many drums a metal hoop, tightened around the top of the instrument, holds the drum head in place.

Sometimes the drum head is secured by gluing it to the frame. It can also be nailed or pegged in place.

# Gongs, Rattles and Bells

There are many percussion instruments on which it is possible to play tunes. Most of these have a set of bars of different lengths, which sound different pitches when they are struck. The bars can be made of wood, metal or even stone. Instruments with wooden bars are called xylophones. Metallaphones have metal bars, and lithophones have stone ones. Other tuned percussion instruments have gongs instead of bars. Gong instruments are an important part of the *gamelan* orchestras of Java and Bali.

Rattles and jingles are simple percussion instruments that come to life when they are shaken. Rattles can be fashioned from a whole range of materials including wood, clay, animal shells and dried seed pods. Jingles are small tinkling bells that are often worn by dancers around their ankles and wrists. Much larger and louder are the struck bells that ring out from temples across the Eastern Asia.

△ Jingles attached to the ankles and arms of this Indian dancer provide a tinkling accompaniment to all her movements.

▽ The stone chime is one of the oldest Chinese instruments, dating back over 7,000 years. The stones are cut into 'L'-shapes of varying thickness so that each one has a different pitch. The stone chime was played at dances, banquets and other ceremonial occasions.

Gong with lowest pitc

Seeds threaded onto net

Hollow gourd

◁ Some rattles are made from dried vegetable shells, or gourds. When this Nigerian rattle is shaken, seeds strung onto a net strike the body of the gourd.

▽ This rattle used by the
Algonquin people of North
America has a body made from a
turtle shell. Used in tribal
ceremonies, the base of the handle
is made from the head of a turtle.

△ Found in Asia and
Europe, the Jew's
harp is played inside
the mouth. Its twangy
sound is made by
plucking the metal
tongue. Changing the
shape of the mouth
alters the pitch.

**Gongs made of bronze**

**Gong with highest pitch**

**Tuned gongs rest on cords**

**Wooden frame**

△ The *bonang* is one of the instruments played in
the Indonesian *gamelan* orchestras. Its chiming gongs,
each tuned to a different pitch, sit on cords attached
to a carved wooden frame. The bronze gongs are
struck with two padded beaters.

▽ Bells in church
towers are rung by
pulling on a rope.
This first pull makes
the bell swing round
on its wheel and ring
out. A second pull
takes the bell back to
its original position.

△ The *sasara* from Japan is a
rattle made of thin pieces of
wood strung onto a cord.
Its noisy clatter is most often
heard with the flute and
drum at village festivals.

# Guitars, Harps and Lutes

The guitar is played all over the world. It can be used to accompany singing or dancing, or it can be played as a solo instrument. Probably introduced into Spain by the Arabs, it was established throughout Europe by the late 1300s. Modern guitars include the folk guitar, classical guitar, flamenco guitar and the electric guitar. But the most ancient string instrument is the musical bow, a single string tied at both ends to a flexible stick, that may be 16,000 years old. Harps and lyres also date back thousands of years – they were first played in Egypt about 5,000 years ago. The lyre survives only in parts of Africa, but the harp is still played around the world.

One very popular instrument in Europe during the 1500s and 1600s was the lute. Today, lutes come in many different shapes and sizes, but they all have a neck joined to a deep resonating belly.

△ The delicate sound of the harp has often been associated with heavenly matters. This golden statue of King David with a harp is based on a story in the Bible.

△ Irish harps were small and light enough to be carried from town to town by wandering minstrels.

▷ The classical guitar is also known as the Spanish guitar. In the late 1800s a Spanish guitar maker, Antonio Torres Juardo, created the basic size and shape of the modern guitar. The Spanish guitarist and composer, Francisco Tárrega, developed present-day guitar-playing methods.

**Fingerboard**

**Metal frets**

**Sound hole allows sound out of the sound chamber**

**Bridge supports the strings and transmits vibrations to the sound board**

**End-block join together the tv side sections**

**Sound board has fan bracing to strengthen guitar**

68

ing head

ut

Neck

## THE EUROPEAN RENAISSANCE LUTE

Throughout the 1500s and 1600s lute makers aimed to make the instrument as light as possible – consequently the bodies of some lutes were only 1mm thick. Many were beautifully decorated with ebony and ivory.

▽ John Williams (born 1941) is an Australian guitarist who plays both classical and jazz music. He studied with the great Spanish guitarist, Andres Segovia. In the late 1970s he formed a pop group, Sky.

**Strings made from nylon**

**Top block joins the neck to the body**

**Rosewood back**

**Maker's label**

▽ Lyres are still widely played in many African countries, often at religious festivals and in magical rites. This large, box-shaped lyre, called a *beganna*, is found only in Ethopia.

**Curved side section**

## LISTEN FOR

LUTE
John Dowland – *Lachrimae*

Johann Sebastian Bach – *Lute Suites*

HARP
Wolfgang Amadeus Mozart – *Flute and Harp Concerto*

GUITAR
Antonio Vivaldi – *Guitar Concertos in A major and D minor*

Manuel De Falla – *Homage for the Tomb of Debussy, Nights in the Gardens of Spain*

Heitor Villa-Lobos – *Preludes*

# Zithers and Fiddles

Some of the most beautiful stringed instruments come from India where the tradition of string-playing goes back many thousands of years. One of the oldest is the *vina*, a type of zither (an instrument with strings running the entire length of the body). According to Indian legend, the *vina* was first made by the god Krishna in the likeness of the goddess Parvati. Its delicate sound is supposed to echo the softness of her breathing.

Zithers are also important in Japan, China and other East Asian countries. The shape of the Japanese *koto* is said to have come from the appearance of a crouching dragon. This instrument has 13 silk strings stretched across a wooden sound box. A similar instrument is also played in China, where it is called a *ch'in*, and in Korea where it is known as a *kayagum*. Board zithers are found throughout Europe. These zithers have strings stretched across a flat or gently curving wooden board.

△ The board zither has been a popular folk instrument in Europe for more than 200 years.

◁ Japan's national instrument is the *koto*. Underneath each of the 13 silk strings is a bridge that can be moved to produce different notes.

**Metal strings**

**Sliding metal rings for fine tuning**

▷ The *vina* has a rounded body carved from wood, with a gourd attached to the hollow neck. This instrument, from southern India, has seven metal strings and 24 brass frets. The strings are plucked with a plectrum, or by long fingernails on the player's right hand.

▷ The Chinese *erhu* is known as the spike fiddle because its long neck pierces the sound box. The bow is threaded through the *erhu's* two strings.

**Wooden sound box, or shell**

**Sound table**

**Decorate sound h**

## THE SARANGI

The *sarangi* is a fiddle from northern India. It usually has three or four main strings and like the *sitar* it also has a set of 'sympathetic' strings. The body of the *sarangi* is hollowed out from a single block of wood. The hollow part is then covered with goatskin or parchment. The *sarangi* is held upright and played with a bow. It is used to accompany singers, and also played as a solo instrument.

**Tuning pegs**

**Brass frets**

**Carved dragon's head peg box**

**Hollow wooden neck**

**Hollow gourd rests on player's left knee and adds extra resonance**

△ The Indian *sitar* player Ravi Shankar (born 1920) is famous for his solo concerts. His recitals in Europe and North America have helped introduce Western audiences to classical Indian music.

**Arched metal frets**

**Sympathetic strings**

◁ The *sitar*, from northern India, is a type of lute that resembles the *vina*. When the player plucks the main strings, a second set of strings known as sympathetic strings vibrates under the frets. This gives the *sitar* its attractive, shimmering sound.

**Sound box made from a gourd**

**Fine-tuning bead**

# Orchestral Strings

The violin is one of the most expressive of all instruments and forms the heart of the Western orchestra. As a solo instrument it is at times sad and soulful, and at other times flamboyant and lively. The sound of many violins played in unison is just as pleasing. The viola is only slightly bigger than the violin, but its tone is deeper and more mellow.

The cello and the double bass form the lower strings in the Western orchestra. Like the violin, the cello's expressive tone makes it an ideal solo instrument. The double bass has its origins in another family of bowed string instruments, the viols, from which it was developed in the 1500s. Measuring 1.8 metres tall, it can be played by plucking the strings as well as using the bow.

△ The classical string quartet dates from the late 1700s when both Haydn and Mozart wrote music to be played informally in people's homes. This is why it is sometimes called chamber music. A classical quartet consists of two violins, a viola and a cello.

▷ Played in Europe during the 1600s and 1700s, the *tromba marina* had only one gut string. The player drew a bow across the top of the instrument, while varying the pitch by stopping the string.

Bow

Bridge

Chinrest

Tailpiece anchors strings to belly

End pin

Back

Sound post

◁ The rock and roll music of Bill Haley and the Comets in the mid-1950s featured a double bass played in an adventurous way!

**Strings made of metal, or gut wound with thin wire**

Peg box

Scroll

Tuning peg

**Fingerboard**

**Horse hair**

◁ The modern violin has more than 70 different parts. Its design is both practical and beautiful. The body resonates the sound, while the narrowing, or waist, at the centre allows the player to reach the highest and lowest strings.

## STRING FAMILY

violin

cello

viola

double bass

double bass    cello    viola    violin

△ Yehudi Menuhin (born 1916) is one of this century's most celebrated violinists. He was only 16 years old when he made a famous recording of Elgar's *Violin Concerto*, with the composer conducting.

◁ The modern design of the cello was established by Antonio Stradivari in the late 1600s.

# Flutes and Recorders

Flutes come in all shapes and sizes, can be made from a number of materials and produce a wide variety of sounds. The haunting whisper of the panpipes is very different from the clear, liquid tones of the orchestral flute. Different again is the simple and unadorned sound of the recorder. Flutes can be found in many forms around the world. There are bamboo flutes in Asia, clay flutes in South America and the orchestral flute in the West. The way a flute is played also varies from one instrument to the next – air can be blown down or across the mouthpiece. Some flutes are even played with breath from the nose!

The orchestral flute is blown sideways, has keys covering its holes and is usually made from metal. The recorder is played downwards, and has open holes that are covered by the player's fingers. Both these instruments have long histories in the West.

△ The panpipes get their name from the ancient Greek god Pan. It was said that Pan was in love with a nymph who, to escape his advances, was changed into a reed. From this reed, Pan made the first panpipes.

**Trill keys**

**Roller and keys for the little finger of the right hand**

**Keys operated by fingers**

**Body joint**

**Hole covered by key**

**Foot joint**

◁ Unusual and beautiful clay whistles were used over a thousand years ago by the peoples of South America. These were often given the form of animals or people.

## THE FLUTE FAMILY

The piccolo is a half-sized flute used for playing high, light notes. It is pitched an octave above the orchestral flute. Both instruments make use of the same fingering.

piccolo

flute

flute    piccolo

◁ Some of the peoples who live in the Amazon rainforest believe that air blown through the nose has magical powers. Nose flutes are also common throughout many Pacific islands.

**Rod mechanism**

**Lip plate**

▽ The modern orchestral flute dates from the 1840s, when German inventor Theobald Boehm changed its shape and system of keys. Most modern flutes are made from metal, but a few players still use wooden flutes.

**Felt or leather pad under each key makes airtight seal with hole**

**Screw end for fine tuning**

**Oval-shaped blow hole**

**Head joint**

△ The Irish flautist James Galway (born 1939) is famed for his fine playing, and best-selling records. Before beginning his solo career in 1973, he was the principal flautist with the Berlin Philharmonic Orchestra.

## DOLMETSCH RECORDER

The recorder was very popular in Europe in the 1500s and 1600s. It was then almost forgotten until the early 1900s, when instrument-maker Arnold Dolmetsch became interested in it. Through an accident, his own recorder was lost. Luckily, he had taken careful measurements, and based a new instrument on the old design! This was the beginning of a revival for the recorder.

## MUSICAL SPY

The *shakuhachi* is an end-blown flute from Japan with five fingerholes. Traditionally many *shakuhachi* players were priests who wore a kind of wickerwork basket over their heads while they played. It is said that these priests were actually spies, working for a secret group. Their identity hidden, they walked the city streets eavesdropping on interesting conversations while playing soft tunes on the *shakuhachi*.

## LISTEN FOR

RECORDER
The recorder features in many Baroque works by Antonio Vivaldi, Alessandro Scarlatti and George Philipp Telemann

FLUTE
Johann Sebastian Bach –
*Suite No. 2 in B minor*

Wolfgang Amadeus Mozart –
*Flute Concerto in G major*

Gabriel Fauré –
*Fantasie*

Claude Debussy –
*Syrinx*

Paul Hindemith –
*Sonata for flute and piano*

PICCOLO
Benjamin Britten –
*Variations on a theme by Purcell*

# Oboes and Clarinets

The oboe and the clarinet are both instruments that use reeds to create air vibrations. The main difference between them is that the oboe has two reeds that vibrate together (a double reed) while the clarinet has a single reed. The oboe has an unmistakable, mournful tone. Its tone is so clear that it plays the note to which all the other members of the orchestra tune their instruments. The clarinet has a smoother, more velvety sound.

Like the flute, relations of the oboe and clarinet are found all over the world. The *shawm* is an ancient double-reed instrument with a loud, shrill sound that is often put to good use at outdoor events. Folk clarinets from the side-blown *bumpa* of Upper Volta to the cane clarinets of South America have also been played for thousands of years.

△ The clarinet, in a variety of forms, has been a popular folk instrument for thousands of years in many different cultures.

## CLARINETS

The bass clarinet is twice as long as the normal clarinet, and it plays notes an octave lower. The top part of the instrument curves over to make it easier to play.

clarinet

bass clarinet

clarinet   bass clarinet

Key

Keys for right hand on middle joint

Lower joint

Flared bell projects sound outwards

Keys for little finger of right hand

△ The *shawm* is a type of ancient folk oboe found throughout parts of Europe, Asia and Africa. The round metal plate below the mouthpiece supports the player's lips.

△ A type of clarinet was first played in Ancient Egypt. The instrument we play today was developed in the 1700s by J. C. Denner of Nuremberg.

Double reed

▽ The first oboe appeared in France in about 1660. It is said that Louis XIV asked the composer Lully and instrument maker Hotteterre to make an indoor *shawm*, and they invented the oboe.

Upper joint

Mouthpiece tapers to fit in player's mouth

Ligature holds single reed

Keys for left hand on head joint

Barrel joint

Rods connect keys

Keys for little finger of left hand

▽ Heinz Holliger (born 1939) is a Swiss oboist and composer who is well known for his experimental work on the oboe. He has pioneered different techniques to achieve new sounds and effects.

◁ The oboe has a double reed (left) which is placed onto a staple, or metal tube. Cork surrounds the staple to ensure a tight fit. Many oboists make their own reeds, carefully scraping the cane until it is exactly the right shape. The clarinet has a single reed (right) which slots into the mouthpiece. A metal band holds the reed in place.

▽ Benny Goodman (1909–1986), an American clarinetist, was famous for playing both jazz and classical music. He commissioned Copland's *Clarinet Concerto*, first performed in 1950.

## OBOE FAMILY

The cor anglais is the tenor version of the oboe. It has a deep plaintive tone. The bassoon has a long conical tube (about three metres) that doubles back on itself.

oboe

cor anglais

bassoon

oboe    cor anglais    bassoon

## LISTEN FOR

OBOE
George Frideric Handel – *Arrival of the Queen of Sheba*

Ludwig van Beethoven – *Symphony No. 6 'Pastoral'*

Edvard Grieg – *Peer Gynt 'Morning'*

Sergei Prokofiev – *Peter and the Wolf*

CLARINET
Wolfgang Amadeus Mozart – *Clarinet Quintet*

Carl Maria von Weber – *Der Freischütz*

Igor Stravinsky – *Ebony Concerto*

Aaron Copland – *Concerto for clarinet, harp and strings*

George Gershwin – *Rhapsody in Blue*

# Saxophones and Bagpipes

The saxophone was invented in the early 1840s, by an instrument-maker called Adolphe Sax. A cross between a woodwind and a brass instrument, it was originally intended for use in military and marching bands. Today, its highly expressive sound is associated most often with jazz music. Although it makes an occasional appearance in the Western orchestra, the saxophone has never become a regular member of the woodwind or brass section.

The bagpipe has a much longer history than the saxophone, dating back some 3,000 years. When the player squeezes the bag, air is pushed out through one or more pipes attached to the bag. Inside the pipes are reeds, which vibrate as the air flows over them. This gives the bagpipe its very distinctive, raucous sound.

△ Traditionally, the bagpipe was played by shepherds and other countryfolk. This woodcarving from the 1400s shows a French bagpiper.

△ Charlie Parker (1920–1955) was a brilliant American jazz saxophonist who played both alto and tenor instruments. His brilliant technique was an important influence on many other jazz musicians.

**Single reed mouthpiece**

▷ The saxophone has a metal body, the mouthpiece of a clarinet, and a flared bell. An accomplished player can make this eloquent instrument sound loud or soft, harsh or smooth.

**Rod mechanism connects keys to pads**

**Key**

**Bell**

**Thumb support**

**Pads close tone holes**

**Melody pipe, or chanter**

## SAXOPHONES

Originally there were 14 different members of the saxophone family. Today, only four saxophones are used regularly.

soprano

alto          baritone

tenor

soprano     alto     tenor     baritone

▽ The *sheng* is a Chinese mouth organ with a reed fitted inside each pipe. The player blows into the mouthpiece and covers a fingerhole to make an individual pipe sound.

▽ The Scottish Highland pipes are among the most well-known type of bagpipe. The tartan-covered bag is inflated by blowing into a mouthpiece. Squeezing the bag sounds the melody pipe, or chanter, and the three drone pipes.

△ This Hungarian bagpipe has a kidskin bag which is pumped up by a set of bellows. The wooden goat's head is also found on other central European bagpipes.

**Bass drone**

**Mouthpipe – player blows in here to inflate bag**

▽ During the 1600s the *musette* became a favoured instrument at the French court. This softly-toned bagpipe has a finely embroidered silk bag, and pipes made from ebony and ivory.

**Tenor drones**

Leather or rubber bag covered with tartan

# *Horns – Ancient and Modern*

The first horns were made from animal horn. By breaking off the horn's tip and blowing down the hole a note could be sounded. Further holes were sometimes drilled into the side of the horn. These were covered and uncovered by the player's fingers to make extra notes. Some early horns were used in Medieval Europe as signalling instruments especially for hunting. When composers such as Lully wrote hunting scenes in their operas, they included the horn's familiar call which effectively introduced the horn into the orchestra. By the late 1700s Mozart was writing concertos for the solo horn and orchestra.

During the 1800s the horn acquired valves which made the instrument easier to play. At the turn of the last century the double, or French, horn was developed and it has since become a standard member of the orchestra.

△ A hunting scene depicted in a French book of the 1400s. French hunting horns were wide enough for the huntsman to wear the horn over his shoulders.

**FRENCH HORN**

The horn is pitched in F and is capable of playing just over two octaves – from F in the bass clef, up to C in the treble clef. In the orchestra, the horn is positioned next to the trumpets and behind the clarinets.

*Wide flaring bell – hand is inserted to adjust pitch and support instrumen*

▷ The lur is a Bronze Age horn found in Scandinavia. Its shape is thought to be based upon a mammoth's horn.

▷ This Italian horn is made from the horn of a goat. The harsh blast of sound produced by these basic horns was used by herdsmen to round up their animals.

**Mouthpiece**

**Thumb lever shuts off section of tubing**

**Slide pull**

## THE SERPENT

The serpent was a huge instrument, over two metres long. It was bent into an 'S'-shape to allow the player to reach its six fingerholes, and was very popular during the 1600s and 1700s. Handel wrote parts for it in his *Water Music* and *Firework Music*.

**Levers operated by fingers of left hand**

◁ This French horn is really two horns in one! The player's left thumb works a valve that allows two sets of tubing to be used. One set of tubes is shorter and used for playing brilliant high notes. The longer set is used for the warm, lower notes.

**Rotary valves controlled by levers**

▽ This Japanese conch trumpet, or *horagai,* was used by Buddhist monks. The use of natural instruments, such as shells or hollow canes, goes back to prehistoric times.

▽ Barry Tuckwell, an Australian-born French horn player, was principal horn with the London Symphony Orchestra, 1955-68. Well known as a soloist, composers such as Thea Musgrave have written works for him.

## LISTEN FOR

HORN

Johann Sebastian Bach –
*The Brandenburg Concertos*

Wolfgang Amadeus Mozart –
*Concerto No.1 in D Major*

Robert Alexander Schumann –
*Konzertstuck*

Benjamin Britten –
*Serenade for Tenor, Horn and Strings*

Felix Mendelssohn –
*A Midsummer Night's Dream*

Pytor Ilyich Tchaikovsky –
*Symphony No.5 (slow movement)*

George Frederick Handel –
*Water Music*

Claude Debussy –
*La Mer*

# Trombones and Trumpets

The shrill sound of the trumpet has long been used to send signals and messages, to frighten enemies in battle and to celebrate rituals and ceremonies. The sound of conch shell trumpets was heard by Captain Cook as he approached the islands of Hawaii in the Pacific. The islanders were trying to scare off his ships with their wild noises! The Romans also knew the value of the trumpet – especially in war. They used a long trumpet called a *cornu* both to direct the movements of their own troops and to strike fear in the enemy.

The trombone first appears in European paintings from about 1460. Early trombones in England were known as sackbuts. Apart from a wider tube and a different mouthpiece, the trombone has changed very little over the centuries. Today, the trombone has a regular place in marching bands, orchestras and in jazz music.

△ A wooden angel trumpeter outside St David's cathedral, South Wales.

**Flared bell**

**Water key**

**Bumper knob protects tubing**

**Outer tube of slide made of thin brass**

**Inner tube of slide made of hard-wearing alloy**

**Slide brace for right hand**

▽ This wooden trumpet comes from Papua New Guinea. The musician blows into the hole bored in its side.

## BRASS FAMILY

trombone

trumpet

trumpet

trombone

The trumpet usually played in bands and orchestras is the B(flat) trumpet. The trombone section usually includes two tenor trombones and one bass trombone.

◁ The modern trumpet has three piston valves. Its length of tubing is curled in on itself to make it easier to carry and play.

**Piston valves**

**Tuning slide changes pitch**

**Cup-shaped mouthpiece**

**Water key releases build-up of condensation**

**Counterweight balances instrument**

**Tuning slide bow**

**Barrel contains spring to cushion impact of slide**

**Brace for left hand**

**Mouthpiece**

◁ The trombone is different from all the other brass instruments in that it has a slide. The player pushes and pulls the slide to change the length of tubing, which in turn changes the pitch.

▽ American trumpeter Miles Davis (1926-1991) was one of the most inventive jazz musicians of all time. He developed bebop and jazz fusion which combined jazz with rock.

◁ The didgeridoo makes a deep, droning sound and is played by the Aborigine people of Australia. The player must breathe in through the nose while blowing down the hollowed out instrument.

83

# Tubas and Bugles

The tuba plays the deepest and the weightiest notes in the brass section of the Western orchestra, and is this section's youngest member. The tuba was first used in military bands in Berlin in the 1830s, only taking its place in the orchestra in the later 1800s. Composers such as Richard Wagner began to use it to add extra power to the bass line. During this period, instrument-makers experimented with many different designs. Perhaps the best-known of these instruments is the sousaphone – a bass tuba with a huge bell. Today, the tuba is still an important member of military bands in Europe and the USA. It is often simply referred to as the 'bass'.

△ The English Coldstream Guards' band on parade. The bold, rousing sound of the tuba and trombone makes them ideally suited to military or marching bands.

*Piston valves open and shut tubing*

◁ The cornet is played in the same way as the trumpet, but it makes a rather more mellow, rounded sound. It is the lead instrument in brass bands.

△ In the 1870s the composer Richard Wagner developed an instrument called a Wagner tuba. Its sound bridged the gap between that of the French horn and the trombone.

## THE BUGLE

The bugle has been a military instrument since the late 1700s, when it was used to send signals in battle and during the army's normal daily routine. The bugle is a small instrument that can be held in one hand as it is played. Military bugles are often decorated with tasselled cords.

**Large flaring bell amplifies sound**

◁ The tuba is both an orchestral and a band instrument. In the orchestra it is held on the player's lap. For marching in a military band, the tuba is rested on the player's shoulder.

**Wide bore gives deep and smooth sound**

**Cup-shaped mouthpiece**

◁ The sousaphone was built in the 1800s for John Philip Sousa, the American bandleader. The bell can be made from fibreglass to reduce weight and make marching with it easier.

◁ Despite its large size, the tuba can produce a surprisingly agile sound. It is normally used, however, to add weight to the bass line in the orchestra, where it can be heard to play its distinctive oom-pah-pahs!

▽ The inspiring Swedish tuba player, Michael Lind, is Director of the first Scandinavian Brass Symposium.

**Slide pull-ring adjusts pitch**

## THE TUBA

There are five different sizes of tuba ranging from the euphonium to the contrabass tuba. The orchestral tuba is the most common. Tubas sit next to the trombone section in the orchestra.

# Keyboard Instruments

Invented over 2,000 years ago, the organ is unique among keyboard instruments. While the strings of the harpsichord are plucked, and those of the piano are struck, the organ is powered by wind. Compressed air flows along its pipes, giving the organ its rich, resonating sound. Depending on the row of pipes played, however, its tones may be reedy or flute-like.

*Two keyboards, or manuals*

The most important of the keyboard instruments during the Baroque and Classical periods was the harpsichord, with its bright, clear sound. It lost some popularity after the 1700s when the pianoforte (or piano) became known. Bartolommeo Cristofori, the piano's inventor, called it a 'harpsichord with loud and soft'. The piano's ability to respond to the touch of the finger gives it great expression, and a 'singing' quality. Its full potential began to be realized from the 1770s when Mozart started to play and compose for it.

△ In this painting from the 1400s, an angel plays a portative organ. The bellows of this small, portable instrument were worked by the player's left hand.

▽ The organ is often called the 'King of instruments' because many examples are so large. The two great eras of organ building took place in North Germany during the 1600s and France during the 1800s.

*Television monitor allows organist to see conductor's beat*

*Stops*

*Set of five manuals*

◁ The organ in Westminster Abbey has five manuals, or keyboards, and over 120 stops. When a stop is pulled out it allows air to flow through a specific set of pipes. Like all modern organs, it is powered by electricity.

*Swell pedals control volume of sound*

*Pedal board operated by player's feet*

◁ Some harpsichords made from the 1670s onwards have two keyboards, or manuals. The strings operated by the keys on the upper manual produce a thinner, lighter sound than those on the lower manual.

**Decorated case and cover**

**Strings supported by wooden bridges**

△ Mitsuko Uchida (born 1948) comes from Tokyo, Japan. She studied the piano in Vienna, and in 1969 she won first prize in the Beethoven competition. She is well-known for her playing of the Mozart piano concertos.

▽ The piano's strings are stretched over an iron frame. Playing the keys causes wooden hammers, padded with felt, to strike the strings. The vibrations from the strings are then amplified by a wooden sound board.

**Cast iron frame**

**Wooden sound board**

**Bass and tenor strings**

**Treble strings**

**Tuning pegs**

**Hammers**

**Keyboard has 88 keys**

## PIANO AND HARPSICHORD

With its seven octaves the piano has a greater range than the harpsichord.

piano

harpsichord

## LISTEN FOR

ORGAN
Johann Sebastian Bach –
*Toccata and Fugue in D minor*

Olivier Messiaen –
*La Nativité du Seigneur*

HARPSICHORD
François Couperin –
*Pieces de Clavécin*

Johann Sebastian Bach –
*Goldberg Variations*

PIANO
Wolfgang Amadeus Mozart –
*Piano Concerto No. 21 in C*

Ludwig van Beethoven –
*Piano Concerto No. 5*

Franz Schubert –
*Moments musicaux*

Robert Schumann –
*Scenes from Childhood*

Alexander Scriabin –
*Piano Sonata No. 5*

# *Electronic Instruments*

◁ Invented in the 1920s, the ondes martenot is played from a keyboard, or by sliding a metal ring along a track. It makes a weird, swooping sound.

Ever since the early years of this century, new instruments have been developed in step with the latest technology. The discovery that air vibrations can be turned into electrical signals has led to the invention of all kinds of musical instruments. These include the rarely heard theremin and ondes martenot as well as the hugely popular electric guitar which was developed in the 1950s. The synthesizer, which first appeared in the 1960s, revolutionized electronic music by allowing musicians to create totally new sounds.

Today one of the most exciting areas of music making lies with the computer. Although the computer itself is not a musical instrument, synthesizers, samplers and sequencers can be connected to it to allow the creation of an endless variety of musical sounds and effects.

Pitch wheel

Strap scre

Solid wooden body

▽ The spooky sound of the theremin is controlled by the position of the player's hands. The instrument was named after its Russian inventor.

Bridge

Fingerpl

Tremolo arm varies pitch

Output socket to amplifier

Control knobs

Pick-ups turn vibrations into electric signals

Back panel contains MIDI and stereo output connections

Display panel

Pre-set and edit buttons control stored sounds and create new ones

◁ The modern synthesizer can reproduce the sound of any instrument or create entirely new ones. The sounds are made by special circuits called oscillators and shaped by other circuits called filters.

Full-size keyboard

▽ The electric guitar has a flat, solid body. Unlike an acoustic guitar, there is no need for a resonator because the vibrations of the strings are picked up and amplified electronically. This guitar is commonly used in rock and pop bands.

Tuning head

*Fender* STRATOCASTER

Metal frets

Fingerboard

Fret position markers

△ Jimi Hendrix (1942-1970) was an American rock musician. He dazzled audiences with his inspired playing of the electric guitar.

Steel strings

### SEMI-ACOUSTIC

The semi-acoustic guitar is a cross between an acoustic guitar and an electric guitar. It has electric pick-ups and a hollow, resonating body. This allows the guitarist to play with or without amplification.

### LISTEN FOR

ELECTRIC GUITAR
Jimi Hendrix – *Purple Haze*

Eric Clapton – *Layla*

Peter Green – *Albatross*

Prince – *Purple Rain*

ONDES MARTENOT
Olivier Messiaen – *Turangalîla-symphonie*

THEREMIN
The Beach Boys – *Good Vibrations*

SYNTHESIZER
Jean-Michel Jarre – *Oxygène*

Kraftwerk – *The Model*

▷ Traditional instruments, as well as synthesizers, can be connected to a computer using MIDI (Musical Instrument Digital Interface) lead. Once stored in the computer's memory the musical sounds can be triggered to produce a whole range of different effects.

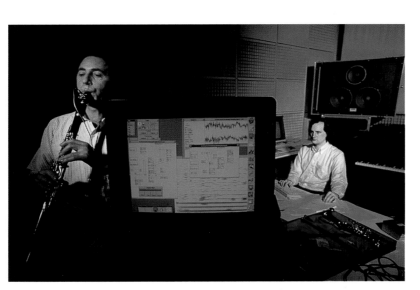

# Playing as a Team

For many people music is a communal activity, whether it is played in a local band or grand symphony orchestra. Being part of a group has its own rewards, but some of the wonder of playing music in a team is that its beauty can be enriched with a range of voices or instruments. The first Western orchestras accompanied singers and consisted only of stringed instruments. The orchestra only really came into its own in the 1700s, when pieces were written especially for it. The new symphonies demanded a greater number of players, leading to the introduction of a conductor to hold everyone together. Even today, however, small orchestras can still be directed by the lead violin.

△ A gathering of musical ladies and gentlemen in 1700s. This kind of music making was popular among the merchant and aristocratic classes.

▽ The conductor interprets the music, deciding on such things as beat, 'phrasing' and tempo. Most conductors use a baton to direct the orchestra.

Tubular bells

Glockenspiel

Snare drum

Celesta

Bass drum

French horns

Trumpets

Clarinets

Piccolo   Flutes

Harp

Piano

Second violins

First violins

▽ A typical orchestra is made up of about twenty different kinds of instrument, which are divided into four main sections – strings, woodwind, brass and percussion. A very large symphony orchestra may have over a hundred players.

**Percussion table holding small percussive instruments**

**Timpani**

**Gong**

**Tuba**

**Trombones**

**Bassoons**

**Contra-bassoon**

**Oboes**

**Cor anglais**

**Violas**

**Cellos**

**Double basses**

△ School orchestras often achieve a very high standard of playing, and perform with success in public.

△ Non-Western orchestras and ensembles have a long history. In this instrumental ensemble from Japan, the drums are positioned in front of the various wind instruments – the opposite of a Western orchestra.

◁ The string section of an orchestra is bigger than the other sections, making up for the soft tone of its instruments. It forms the heart of the orchestra and is composed of violins, violas, cellos and double basses. The violins play in two groups: the first violins play the highest pitched part of the music, the second violins the next highest.

# Amateur Music Making

All over the world there are talented musicians – performing formally or informally, by themselves or in groups – who make music just for the love of it. Such musicians are known as amateurs. Unlike their professional counterparts who have the pressure of earning a living through their art, amateurs are able to play for sheer joy. Some amateurs, however, rank among the world's best musicians. The London Bach Choir, for example, sings alongside top professional orchestras.

Other amateurs take a more low-key approach. They are happy to sing or play in village halls or squares, or in bars and cafés. Many schools and youth groups encourage young talent by putting on their own musical performances, while local music competitions are popular with both young and older amateurs.

Street musicians cross the boundaries between amateur and professional. The magic of an unexpected tune played by a busker can brighten up a gloomy city subway. Even the busy commuter might stop and listen for a while, showing his or her pleasure by giving money.

△ A mother teaches her son to play the hurdy-gurdy. Traditionally, musical skills were handed down the generations by parents to children.

▷ Students playing in a string quartet bring music to a busy Dublin street. Onlookers show their appreciation by dropping money into the open cello case.

Prince Albert plays the harmonium to Queen Victoria and the German composer Felix Mendelssohn. Other gifted amateurs with royal connections include King David in the Old Testament, King Henry VIII of England and Frederick the Great of Prussia. Among non-royal amateurs, the Russian scientist and composer Alexander Borodin is one of the most well-known.

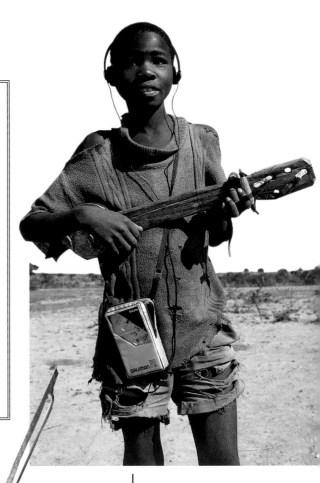

△ A young African boy strums a home-made guitar while listening to music on his personal stereo.

◁ The Japanese violinist Shinichi Suzuki believed that the best way for young people to learn an instrument is to play together. Today, thousands of children learn the violin using the Suzuki method.

# The Power of Music

△ In Ancient Egypt music was important for entertainment and religious ritual. Here, musicians entertain guests at a banquet. One plays a flute while the other claps.

Music is such a powerful force that, according to many legends, it was created by the gods themselves. One of the myths of the ancient Greeks tells how Orpheus was given the gift of music by the gods. He played his lyre so beautifully that he could charm the trees, the mountains and even the wild beasts with his music. While such myths celebrate the heavenly origins of sound, other myths celebrate its creative power. Sometimes the sound described is a howl or a word, sometimes it is music. A Polynesian chant relates how the world was created through the songs of the god Taaroa.

In the past, people often called upon the magic strength of music to aid them in their everyday lives. There are work songs for all times of the farming year, as well as songs sung by shepherds or cowherds to their animals. Sometimes, though, work songs had a more practical purpose. For example, sailors heaving on a rope used the rhythm of a shanty to help them pull together.

In some cultures music has traditionally been used to treat and relieve distress and illness. Healing through music is now becoming more common in modern medicine.

◁ A sailor dances the hornpipe to the accompaniment of a violin. As well as enjoying music and dances in their free time, sailors also had a range of songs to help them while they worked onboard ship.

◁ Shamans, or witch-doctors, use the energy of music and dance to enter a trance-like state. Shamans believe that in this state they are able to bring some of the powers of the spirit world to the human one.

## MUSIC THERAPY

Music therapy is a way of using music to help people. Here, a child with disabilities explores his feelings through the experience of playing a drum.

People who have difficulty communicating in words often find that they can express themselves more freely by making music. This can help them to cope more effectively with their day to day lives.

▷ A Dinka man from southern Sudan bangs a slit drum while telling a story. In many cultures, stories are accompanied by music making.

# Dance

Dancing is one of the oldest and most expressive forms of communication. Since the earliest times dance, like music, has been closely linked to the rhythms of everyday life. Through sound and movement, early peoples praised their gods, and tried to understand the world around them. The major events of life – birth, death, the changing of the seasons, the coming of spring, seed time and harvest – were all celebrated by ritual dancing. There were also dances for special occasions, such as when war broke out, a successful hunt or praying to the gods for rain.

In some cultures, ritual dances continue to play a very important part. Even in Europe, people still perform dances, such as the Maypole celebration, which have their origins in traditions that are thousands of years old.

All around the world people dance for pleasure. Ballroom dancing, the waltz, the foxtrot, tap and many Latin American dances have specific steps and rhythms. Other dances have a much freer range of movements and expression. Dancing can also be used to tell stories. In India, many dances act out legends, myths and historical events. Classical ballet, too, is based on story telling as are the Japanese dance dramas, *No* and *kabuki*.

△ The Hindu god, Shiva, performs the dance of creation and destruction at the centre of the Universe. Shiva is also known as Sri Nataraja, Lord of the Dance.

◁ The tradition of Maypole dancing still continues in parts of Europe. The origin of the Maypole is thought to be the mythical Tree of Life that linked Earth with Heaven, and the gods above. The dance was originally part of a spring fertility ritual, ensuring healthy crops and a good harvest later in the year.

◁ The Leopard dance is a ceremonial hunting dance of the Bapende people of Zaire. Their masks and costumes symbolize the leopard.

◁ Modern dance has done away with many of the postures and traditions of Classical ballet. Often, a modern dance does not relate a particular story, but aims to evoke a certain mood or feeling.

## CLASSICAL BALLET

The styles and traditions of ballet grew out of the dances of the European courts, beginning in Italy in the 1400s. Ballet dancers learned to keep their bodies still while extending their arms and legs in elegant, formal movements. In the 1800s, Romantic ballets told stories of delicate, make-believe creatures. Dancers depicted these with quick, light movements performed on tiptoe. The scene below comes from the Classical ballet, *Swan Lake*, whose music was composed by Tchaikovsky. Through their expressive movements, the dancers tell the story of Prince Siegfried, and the Swan Princess.

# *The Music Industry*

△ The programme for an 1814 performance in Vienna of Ludwig van Beethoven's only opera – *Fidelio*.

▽ Performers such as the Irish band U2 require an army of assistants to organize publicity, travel and security when they are on tour.

Music is for enjoyment, but it is also one of the biggest industries in the world and is worth billions of pounds a year. It needs writers and performers, administrators and manufacturers to supply and run it. Composers earn money when their music is played, musicians and record companies make money when CDs (compact discs) and singles are sold. Impresarios, people who organize live performances, make their profit through ticket sales.

Concerts help to promote the performers and their music. This helps to sell records which provides profit for the record companies, musicians and writers. Skilled technicians and managers are essential for the success of a concert which also needs to be organized, advertized and administered. Concerts can take place anywhere from arts centres such as the Lincoln Center in New York to sporting arenas such as Wembley Stadium in London.

Most of the world's big cities have annual festivals of classical, opera, rock, jazz, folk or world music. These festivals can be sponsored by private or commercial donations. Investing in live performances is becoming a very important part of the music industry.

△ Film soundtracks and songs are a major part of the music industry. The Indian film industry, based in Bombay and generally known as Bollywood, produces hundreds of musicals a year.

△ The Bregenz Festival in Austria features large-scale opera productions, such as *Fidelio*, on a floating stage. Over recent years, opera has become hugely popular, with lavish performances and huge audiences.

◁ Writing for the cinema and television brings the music of a composer such as Michael Nyman to the attention of a very wide audience.

# Recording and Broadcasting

The first sound recording was made in 1877 by Thomas Edison, an American inventor. His machine, called a phonograph, stored sound on a cylinder covered with tin foil. Ten years later, Emile Berliner made a breakthrough with the invention of the gramophone which recorded and played back sound on shellac discs. These not only sounded better but also lasted longer than cylinders.

In the 1880s Heinrich Hertz and Guglielmo Marconi learned how to control radio waves. However, it was not until the development of the radio valve in 1906, by Edison among others, that radio broadcasting became realistic. By the 1920s most countries had their own radio stations which created a huge new audience for performers and composers.

In 1948 long playing (LP) vinyl records appeared. These could store much more sound than the old shellac discs and the quality was better. Since the 1980s digital technology has revolutionised sound–recording. Compact discs, mini discs and digital audio tapes (DAT) have replaced vinyl.

△ Thomas Edison originally intended his phonograph, an early version of the record player, to be used as an office dictating machine.

▽ Radio valves, which made radio sound a commercial possibility, were developed from electric light bulbs. They converted radio waves into electric current.

△ In a recording session, the performer plays in a soundproof studio. The music is usually recorded in separate 'takes' by the recording engineer.

**Digital compact cassette**

▷ Over the last hundred years recording quality has improved enormously from the scratchy sound of the old 78s to the crystal clear quality of compact discs. Audio tapes recorded digitally (DAT) are also of a higher quality.

**Mini disc**

**Digital audio tape**

◁ Events such as the Live Aid concert (1985) are broadcast around the world with the use of communication satellites. Relays from country to country once required a chain of transmitters. Today radio and television signals are beamed up to satellites.

*Until the 1940s records were made of a brittle material called shellac*

*Some singles were produced in limited numbers on special coloured vinyl*

*A single is played at 45 revolutions per minute*

*The LP (long player) is played at 33⅓ revolutions per minute*

*CDs (compact discs) are metallic engraved discs which can be read by a laser beam*

*Blank audio cassette*

*Pre-recorded cassette*

# Buildings for Music

Churches were among the first public buildings in which music could be heard by large numbers of people. The first theatre was built for the purpose of performing non-religious opera and was opened in Venice, Italy, in 1637. Before this time, opera had only been seen in the palaces and courts of Europe. The idea quickly caught on – twelve more opera houses were built in Venice by the end of the 1600s!

Small public concert halls for the paying public began to open during the 1700s. These became grander and larger in the 1800s to accommodate the growing audiences and orchestras of the day. Today, modern concert halls must be adaptable for all kinds of music including jazz, classical and pop.

△ J. S. Bach worked for over 25 years at the church of St Thomas in Leipzig, Germany. His works took into account the building's acoustics.

**BUILDINGS ON FIRE!**

The opera house in Covent Garden, London, burning to the ground in 1856. Fire had previously destroyed it in 1808. Fire was a constant hazard in theatres until the late 1800s, and music-lovers would go to shows or concerts at their own risk. There were over a thousand major theatre fires between 1700 and 1800 – the average length of time a theatre stood before being gutted by fire was a mere 18 years! The number of fires decreased when electric lighting replaced gas lamps.

The Metropolitan Opera House in New York opened in 1966 as part of the Lincoln Center for the Performing Arts. It has an auditorium designed in the traditional horseshoe shape that dates back to some of the earliest opera houses. You can see – **1** the auditorium which seats 3,800 people; **2** the orchestra pit; **3** the main stage; **4** the stage manager's desk; **5** and **6** scenery ready to be moved on to the main stage; **7** electrically controlled fly system for hanging backdrops to the main stage; **8** catwalks giving access to stage lighting; **9** strip lights extending across the main stage; **10** the loading bay; **11** dressing rooms; **12** the wardrobe; **13** the carpenters' work area; **14** the paint shop.

Buildings for music come in all shapes and sizes, from small concert rooms suitable for chamber music to huge opera houses.

△ The Opéra in Paris, France, opened in 1875. Built in the grandest style, it can seat over 2,000 people.

△ The shell-shaped roof of the Sydney Opera House is one of the world's best known landmarks.

△ The Albert Hall in London houses the famous Prom concerts every summer.

△ The opera house in Manaus, Brazil stands deep in the rainforest. It was opened in 1896.

# Lives of Composers

△ *Title page from one of Bach's cantatas*

## ADAMS, JOHN
**(1947- )** American, born in Massachusetts. He studied at Harvard University and taught at the San Francisco Conservatory. His compositions, mainly in the minimalist style, include works for strings and full orchestra as well as a three-act opera *Nixon in China*.

## BACH, JOHANN SEBASTIAN (1685-1750)
German, born in Eisenach. Bach is the best-known member of a remarkable family of musicians. He was orphaned young and brought up by his elder brother, a church organist. He worked as a musician at the courts of Weimar and Köthen before becoming choirmaster of the St Thomas Church and School in Leipzig. Here he remained for nearly 30 years, producing a vast amount of music, including religious pieces, such as the *St Matthew Passion*, and music for choir, organ, orchestra and keyboard instruments. He married twice and had twenty children. Four of his sons became well-known musicians and composers.

## BARTÓK, BÉLA (1881-1945)
Hungarian, born in Sinnicolau Mare. He was taught to play the piano by his mother before studying in Bratislava. He was a gifted pianist and many of his piano works were written for him to play himself. Bartók took a particular interest in Hungarian folk music, and this influenced many of his compositions. In 1940 he moved to the USA where he spent five busy but unhappy years before dying in poverty.

△ *Ludwig van Beethoven*

## BEETHOVEN, LUDWIG VAN (1770-1827)
German, born in Bonn. Beethoven first studied music with his father, a singer at the court of the Elector of Cologne, and later with Haydn and he soon became famous as the greatest pianist of his time. Although he was a brilliant composer, he never found composing easy. At the age of 32 he began to go deaf, but he continued to compose, producing the *Eroica* symphony in 1804 and the opera *Fidelio* the following year. Remarkably he wrote some of his best works after he had become completely deaf at the age of 50. Beethoven spent most of his adult life in Vienna, supported by a number of aristocratic patrons. Before his death, his fame had spread throughout Europe.

## BERG, ALBAN
**(1885-1935)** Austrian, born in Vienna. He studied with Schoenberg, who had a major influence on his music. One of Berg's best-known works, the opera *Lulu*, was still unfinished at his death.

▷ *Hector Berlioz*

## BERLIOZ, HECTOR
**(1803-69)** French, born near Grenoble. The son of a doctor, Berlioz studied medicine before taking up music as a career. His music was influenced by the plays of Shakespeare, Romantic poets and Beethoven's symphonies. He never achieved acclaim in France and had to make his living as a music critic.

## BERNSTEIN, LEONARD
**(1918-90)** American, born in Massachusetts. Equally gifted as a conductor, composer and pianist, Bernstein conducted the New York Philharmonic Orchestra from 1958 to 1969. His works span both popular and classical music. They include three symphonies as well as successful Broadway musicals – notably the ever-popular *West Side Story*.

## BIZET, GEORGES
**(1838-75)** French, born in Paris. Bizet entered the Paris Conservatory at nine. He wrote his first symphony in 1855, although it was not performed until 1935. He wrote several

unsuccessful operas, then completed his masterpiece, *Carmen*, just before his early death from heart disease.

## BOULEZ, PIERRE (1925- )
French, born in Montbrison. He studied with Messiaen at the Paris Conservatory. He became one of the leading avant-garde composers of the 1950s. Boulez is also well known as a conductor.

### BRAHMS, JOHANNES (1833-97)
German, born in Hamburg. Brahms was the son of a poor double-bass player. When young, he played the piano in inns and dance-halls to pay for his musical tuition. Brahms produced a large body of music in most fields except opera, but is best known for his symphonies and concertos.

### BRITTEN, BENJAMIN (1913-76)
English, born in Lowestoft. Britten began composing at the age of five. His first opera *Peter Grimes*, was produced in 1945. Britten wrote several pieces for young people including *The Young Person's Guide to the Orchestra*.

### BYRD, WILLIAM (1543-1623)
English, probably born in Lincoln. He was a pupil of Tallis and in 1572 became organist at the Chapel Royal, London. In 1575 Queen Elizabeth I granted Byrd and Tallis a special license to print music. For 21 years only they were allowed to print music in England. Byrd, who wrote sacred music, songs and keyboard music, is often described as 'the father of English music'.

△ *Johannes Brahms*

### CAGE, JOHN (1912-92)
American, born in Los Angeles. He studied with Schoenberg. Always exploring new ideas, Cage invented the 'prepared piano' – a piano with objects such as screws and paper placed on the strings to distort the sound. One of his most famous works *4' 33"*, consists of four minutes and 33 seconds of silence. Cage was also an expert on fungi.

### CARTER, ELLIOTT (1908- )
American, born in New York. He studied at Harvard and with Nadia Boulanger in Paris. He has taught music at Columbia and Yale Universities and has written symphonies, concertos, ballets and chamber music.

### CHOPIN, FREDERIC (1810-49)
Polish, born near Warsaw. Chopin was nine when he first played the piano in public. By the age of 16 he had composed several piano works. He moved to Paris in 1831 and quickly became famous as a teacher and composer. Chopin was also known for his good looks. He fell in love with the French woman-novelist George Sand, who nursed him when he became ill with tuberculosis. They parted in 1848, and he died the following year after touring Great Britain.

### COPLAND, AARON (1900-1990)
American, born in Brooklyn, New York. The young Copland studied in France with the influential teacher Nadia Boulanger. His most famous works are his ballets, such as *Appalachian Spring*, which draw on traditional American music. He also composed operas, symphonies and film scores.

### COUPERIN, FRANÇOIS (1668-1733)
French, born in Paris. Couperin was born into a musical family. His father was organist at the church of St Gervais, Paris, as were nine other Couperins including François himself. Couperin became organist and harpsichordist to King Louis XIV. His work had an influence on Bach.

### DEBUSSY, CLAUDE (1862-1918)
French, born in St Germain-en-Laye, near Paris. His early work was influenced by Wagner, and also by Javanese *gamelan* music. Later compositions have been described as the musical equivalent of Impressionist paintings – pictures in sound. As well as many works for orchestra, such as *La Mer*, Debussy wrote piano music, several ballets and the opera *Pelléas et Mélisande*.

▽ *Aaron Copland*

## DELIUS, FREDERICK (1862–1934)
English, born in Bradford. Delius went to Europe to study music in Leipzig and became friendly with Grieg. From 1890 he lived in France, where he wrote orchestral music and operas. Although he went blind in 1924, he continued to compose until his death.

△ *Frederick Delius*

## DESPREZ, JOSQUIN (1440–1521)
French, born in Beaurevoir, Picardy. Desprez (or Josquin as he was often called) was one of the greatest Renaissance composers. He travelled in Italy as a young man and worked for Cardinal Sforza and the Duke of Ferrara. Later he went to live in France. His works, which include masses and motets, were forgotten after his death but rediscovered in the 1700s.

## DVOŘÁK, ANTONIN (1841–1904)
Czech, born near Prague. Dvořák's father was a butcher and Dvořák was a butcher's boy before studying music and the viola at the Prague Organ School. He worked as an orchestra musician, before Brahms helped him to concentrate on composing. Along with Janáček he helped to develop Czech music. In 1892, however, he went to the USA, and out of homesickness wrote his most famous symphony, *From the New World*. He returned to Prague in 1895.

## ELGAR, EDWARD (1857–1934)
English, born near Worcester. Elgar was the son of an organist and music dealer. He was mainly self-taught and worked locally as a violinist, organist, teacher and conductor. His *Enigma Variations* brought success as a composer when he was 42, and in 1901 his *Pomp and Circumstance March No. 1* became a popular piece. Elgar was one of the first composers to make gramophone recordings, but he wrote little after his wife's death in 1920.

## FAURÉ, GABRIEL (1845–1924)
French, born in Pamiers. Fauré trained as a pianist and organist under Saint-Saëns, and for much of his life worked as a church musician. In 1905 he became director of the Paris Conservatory, where his pupils included Ravel. Fauré is best known for his songs and his *Requiem*, but also wrote chamber music and operas. He was troubled by deafness for the last 20 years of his life.

## GERSHWIN, GEORGE (1898–1937)
American, born in New York. Gershwin, a talented songwriter, first became famous for his Broadway musicals. Most had lyrics by his brother, Ira. In 1924 his *Rhapsody in Blue* for piano and jazz band brought him success as a serious composer. This was followed by the popular 'folk opera' *Porgy and Bess*.

△ *George Gershwin*

## GLASS, PHILIP (1937– )
American, born in Baltimore. The son of a music shop owner, Glass studied at New York's Juilliard School and in Paris. He also worked with the Indian *sitar* player, Ravi Shankar. Glass became famous with his 1976 minimalist-style opera *Einstein on the Beach*.

## GÓRECKI, HENRYK (1933– )
Polish, born near Katowice. Górecki studied at the Katowice Conservatory and with Messiaen in Paris. His works are strongly influenced by Polish religious music. Górecki was virtually unknown outside Poland until the 1992 recording of his *Symphony No 3* achieved world-wide success, selling over a million copies.

◁ *A plaque to mark the birthplace of Edvard Grieg in Bergen, Norway*

## GRIEG, EDVARD (1843-1907) Norwegian, born in Bergen. Grieg was taught by his mother, a pianist, before going on to study at the Leipzig Conservatory. He became very interested in the traditions of Norwegian folk music. His best-known work is his incidental music for *Peer Gynt*, a play by Henrik Ibsen.

## HANDEL, GEORGE FRIDERIC (1685-1759) German-English, born in Halle. The son of a barber-surgeon, Handel became organist of Halle cathedral while still studying law at university. He was a musician in an opera orchestra, then spent four years in Italy, where he wrote several operas. He then worked for the Elector of Hanover, who later became George I of England. After several visits to England in the early 1700s, Handel moved there permanently, working in the courts of Queen Anne and George I. He was a prolific composer, writing *The Messiah* (with its famous Hallelujah Chorus), the *St John Passion*, orchestral pieces such as his *Water Music* and *Music for the Royal Fireworks* and over 40 operas. He died after fainting during a performance of *The Messiah*, and was buried in Westminster Abbey.

## HAYDN, FRANZ JOSEPH (1732-1809) Austrian, born in Rohrau. Haydn, the son of a wheelwright, was a choirboy at St Stephen's Cathedral, Vienna. For much of his career he was musical director to the Esterházys, one of the most powerful families in Hungary. In the 1780s Haydn twice visited England, where his music was very popular, and was made a Doctor of Music of Oxford University. He taught Beethoven and was friends with Mozart. He wrote a huge amount of music of all kinds, including 18 operas and 84 string quartets. However, he is best known for his work in developing the symphony as a musical form. He wrote 104 symphonies, and has been called the 'father of the symphony'.

## HILDEGARD OF BINGEN (1098-1179) German, born in Bemersheim. Hildegard, an abbess, was one of the most famous and remarkable women of her day. She was a gifted composer of sacred music and also a poet, naturalist and mystic.

## HOLST, GUSTAV (1874-1934) English, born in Cheltenham. Holst studied at the Royal College of Music in London. He worked as a trombonist and became director of music at St Paul's Girls' School, London. He had a deep interest in English folk songs. Holst's most famous work is the orchestral suite *The Planets*.

## KODÁLY, ZOLTÁN (1882-1967) Hungarian, born in Kecskemét. Kodály studied at the Liszt Academy of Music and later taught composition there. With Béla Bartók, who was a life-long friend, he began collecting Hungarian folk songs. After Bartók's death in 1945, Kodály was celebrated as Hungary's greatest living composer. Many of his choral works were written for children.

▷ *Franz Liszt*

## LISZT, FRANZ (1811-86) Hungarian, born in Raiding. Liszt, a brilliant pianist and a great showman, first performed in public aged nine. Until 1847 he travelled throughout Europe, giving the concerts that made him famous. Then he became music director at the court of Weimar in Germany. Liszt's works for the piano include his *20 Hungarian Rhapsodies,* and some of his piano compositions rank among the most difficult ever written. At the end of his life he lived in Rome and became deeply religious. One of his daughters, Cosima, married the composer Wagner.

## MACHAUT, GUILLAUME DE (C.1300-77) French, born in Rheims. Machaut was a priest and poet who worked at the courts of John of Luxemburg, the Duchess of Normandy and John, Duke of Berry. His works include both sacred music and songs, many of which are settings for his own poems.

# LIVES OF COMPOSERS

## MAHLER, GUSTAV (1860-1911)
Austrian, born in Kalist, now in the Czech Republic. Mahler studied composition and conducting at the Vienna Conservatory. He held important conducting posts in several European opera houses, such as Budapest, Hamburg and Vienna. Generally, he used to conduct in the winter and then retreat to the mountains of southern Austria during the summer to compose. He is best known as a composer of symphonies and songs. After 1907 he became conductor of the New York Metropolitan Opera, and then of the New York Philharmonic Orchestra. He returned to Vienna in 1911 because of ill-health, and died of pneumonia aged 49.

## MENDELSSOHN, FELIX (1809-47)
German, born in Hamburg. Mendelssohn came from a rich and cultured banking family. He was a gifted pianist as well as a composer; he formed an orchestra when he was 12, and he wrote many works while still in his teens. A journey in 1829 to Scotland inspired his *Hebrides Overture*. His beloved sister, Fanny, was also a composer; after her death, he suffered a series of strokes and died when only 38 years old.

## MONTEVERDI, CLAUDIO (1567-1643)
Italian, born in Cremona. Monteverdi studied the violin and composition at Cremona cathedral and became a court musician to the Duke of Mantua. After the Duke's death he was appointed music director of St Mark's Cathedral, Venice, and became a priest at the age of 65. One of the most inventive of all composers, he helped to develop opera as a musical form. However, only three of his operas survive complete, including *Incoronazione de Poppea*. He also wrote sacred music and songs.

## MOZART, WOLFGANG AMADEUS (1756-91)
Austrian, born in Salzburg. Mozart was the son of the violinist and composer Leopold Mozart. He was a musical prodigy who was already composing at the age of five and played the violin for the Empress of Austria at six. During his childhood, he and his sister toured Europe giving concerts at many royal courts. In adult life, Mozart was less successful. He worked for the Archbishop of Salzburg but often quarrelled with his employer and eventually moved to Vienna. Here he worked as a freelance music teacher, musician and composer, and he married the singer Constanze Weber. During his short life he composed a huge amount of music, operas, masses, oratorios, nearly 50 symphonies, concertos and chamber music. In spite of the success of his operas – such as *The Marriage of Figaro, Don Giovanni, Così Fan Tutte* and *The Magic Flute* – he struggled to make a living and was often in debt. He died from a mysterious illness, possibly typhus, at the age of 35. It has been suggested that he was poisoned by a jealous rival composer, Antonio Salieri, but this is almost certainly untrue.

△ *Mozart's house*

## MUSSORGSKY, MODEST (1839-81)
Russian, born in St Petersburg. Mussorgsky intended to be a soldier but nervous problems made him resign his army commission. He then concentrated on composing, influenced by Rimsky-Korsakov. Mussorgsky's finest compositions are his operas, which include *Boris Godunov*, but much of his work remained unfinished because of his lifelong habit of heavy drinking. This also resulted in his early death.

## PROKOFIEV, SERGEY (1891-1953)
Russian, born in Sontsovska, Ukraine. Encouraged by his mother, a gifted pianist, Prokofiev studied at the St Petersburg Conservatory, where his teachers included Rimsky-Korsakov. He had a reputation as an ultra-modernist rebel.

△ *Modest Mussorgsky, who died aged only 42*

△ *Sergey Prokofiev at the pia*

was written for a competition while he was still a student. He later became the most successful opera composer of his time, and his works are still enormously popular. They include *La Bohème, Madame Butterfly* and *Turandot*.

### PURCELL, HENRY (1659-95)
English, born in London. Purcell's father was a court musician, and Purcell was a chorister of the Chapel Royal and an organist at Westminster Abbey. He then held a series of court appointments under Charles II, James II and William III. His varied musical output is celebrated for its sparkling originality. It includes sacred music, songs, instrumental music and music for stage plays. His brother Daniel was also a composer.

### RACHMANINOV, SERGEY (1873-1943)
Russian, born in Nizhniy Novgorod. Rachmaninov studied piano and composition at the Moscow Conservatory and toured Europe as a pianist, becoming famous for his great virtuoso gifts. In 1917 he left Russia and moved to the USA. He is best known for his piano concertos.

### RAVEL, MAURICE (1875-1937)
French, born near St Jean de Luz. A gifted pianist, Ravel studied at the Paris Conservatory and was influenced by Satie as well as by Eastern music, folk music and jazz. His delicately balanced music is often compared with that of Debussy. He wrote operas, ballets (such as *Bolero*) and piano music.

△ *Henry Purcell as choirboy*

### RIMSKY-KORSAKOV, NIKOLAI (1844-1908)
Russian, born in Tikhvin. Rimsky-Korsakov was a naval officer before becoming a composer, and wrote his first symphony while still in the navy. He then became a professor at the St Petersburg Conservatory. He wrote 16 operas, the orchestral suite *Scheherazade*, chamber music and songs. One of his best-loved pieces is *The Flight of the Bumble Bee* from the opera *The Legend of the Tsar Sultan*.

### RODRIGO, JOAQÚIN (1902- )
Spanish, born in Sagunto. Spain's leading composer of the 1900s went blind at the age of three. He studied in Valencia, then in Paris in 1927. He became famous with his *Concierto de Aranjuez*, in which guitar and orchestra powerfully evoke the landscape of Spain. He later became Professor of Musical History at Madrid University.

### ROSSINI, GIOACHINO (1792-1868)
Italian, born in Pesaro. Rossini's father was a horn player and his mother a singer. He sang in opera as a child and later became director of opera theatres in Naples and Paris. He wrote 36 operas in 19 years, including *The Barber of Seville* – a failure at first but soon hailed as a masterpiece. Then he stopped composing and wrote no more operas during the last 40 years of his life.

### SAINT-SAËNS, CAMILLE (1835- 1921)
French, born in Paris. As a very young child, Saint-Saëns showed exceptional gifts as pianist. He studied at the Paris

△ *Camille Saint-Saëns*

Conservatory and wrote his first symphony at 17. He was soon considered one of the rebels of French music. He taught music as well as writing several operas, symphonies (the *Organ Symphony* is the most famous) and pieces for piano and orchestra. His best-known piece, *Carnival of Animals*, was originally written as a joke.

---

He left Russia in 1918 and lived in England, France, Japan and the USA, but returned to the Soviet Union in 1934. He lived in Moscow for the rest of his life, dying on the same day as the Soviet dictator Joseph Stalin.

### PUCCINI, GIACOMO (1858-1924)
Italian, born in Lucca. Puccini came from a family of professional musicians and worked as a church organist from the age of 14. Later he studied composition at the Milan Conservatory. His first opera

# LIVES OF COMPOSERS

## SATIE, ERIK
**(1866-1925)** French, born in Honfleur. Both of Satie's parents were composers, and he studied at the Paris Conservatory. Best known for his witty piano pieces and ballets.

## SCHOENBERG, ARNOLD (1874-1951)
Austro-Hungarian, born in Vienna. Schoenberg was mainly self-taught. He was helped by the composer Zemlinsky, whose sister he married. Schoenberg developed the 'twelve note' method of composing, which had an important influence on modern music.

## SCHUBERT, FRANZ
**(1797-1828)** Austrian, born in Vienna. The son of a schoolmaster, Schubert learnt several instruments as a child and went to Vienna's Royal Chapel choir school. Schubert was a great admirer of Beethoven and often visited the same coffee house, but was too shy to introduce himself. Before his early death, he produced a large amount of music. He wrote symphonies and chamber music, such as the *Trout Quintet*, but during his lifetime he was best known for his numerous songs.

## SCHUMANN, ROBERT
**(1810-56)** German, born in Zwickau. The son of a bookseller, Schumann studied law before taking piano lessons with Frederick Wieck, his future father-in-law. He composed symphonies, chamber music and over 250 songs. He suffered from mental illness and in 1854 entered an asylum, where he died.

## SHOSTAKOVICH, DMITRI (1906-75)
Russian, born in St Petersburg. Shostakovich studied with his mother, a professional pianist,

△ *Erik Satie*

and then at the Petrograd Conservatory. His *Symphony No 1* made him famous at the age of 21. After his opera *The Lady Macbeth of the Mtsensk District* was strongly criticized in the Soviet press, he concentrated on composing orchestral pieces, concertos and chamber music. During the siege of Leningrad (St Petersburg) by the Germans during World War II, he wrote the *7th* or *Leningrad Symphony*, seen at the time as a symbol of freedom.

## SIBELIUS, JEAN
**(1865-1957)** Finnish, born in Hämeenlinna. The son of a surgeon, Sibelius studied law before entering the Helsinki Conservatory. His works, based on Finnish mythology, soon made him famous. He wrote symphonies, symphonic poems (including *Finlandia*)

and chamber music. In 1931 Sibelius, dissatisfied with his work, stopped composing altogether.

## STOCKHAUSEN, KARLHEINZ
**(1928- )** German, born near Cologne. After living through the traumatic years of World War II, in which he lost both his parents, Stockhausen studied in Cologne and Paris. He became famous for his challenging modern music in the 1950s, and his electronic music has influenced classical composers and rock musicians.

## STRAUSS, JOHANN
**(1825-99)** Austrian, born in Vienna. Strauss, called 'the younger', was the son of composer and conductor Johann Strauss ('the elder') who developed the Viennese waltz. Strauss 'the younger' formed his own orchestra and wrote many famous waltzes, such as *The Blue Danube*. He also wrote 16 operettas.

## STRAUSS, RICHARD
**(1864-1949)** German, born in Munich. Richard Strauss was taught music by his father, first horn player in the Munich court opera. He started composing at six and had several works performed before he was 20. He went on to become a leading opera conductor, working in many of the world's great opera houses. As well as operas, he wrote symphonic poems and songs, including the great *Four Last Songs*.

## STRAVINSKY, IGOR
**(1882-1971)** Russian, born near St Petersburg. The son of an opera singer, Stravinsky was influenced by Debussy.

He is best known for his ballets, such as *The Firebird* and *The Rite of Spring*, which he wrote for the Ballets Russes, the exciting Russian ballet company of the early 1900s. He also wrote operas, orchestral and choral music. He left Russia in 1914 and lived in Switzerland and France before settling in the USA after 1939.

## TALLIS, THOMAS
**(1505-85)** English, probably born in London. From 1540 Tallis worked for the English royal household as a singer and organist. He wrote a large amount of church music, as well as keyboard music.

## TCHAIKOVSKY, PYOTR ILYICH (1840-93)
Russian, born in Kamsko-Vokinsk. Tchaikovsky gave up his job in the civil service to study music at the St Petersburg Conservatory. His music quickly became popular both in Russia and abroad. Tchaikovsky's private life was less happy and, though he is said to have died of cholera, he may have committed suicide. He wrote eleven operas, six symphonies and three ballets – *Swan Lake*, *The Sleeping Beauty* and *The Nutcracker*.

## TIPPETT, MICHAEL
(1905– ) English, born in London. Having played the piano since the age of five, Tippett studied at the Royal College of Music, London. His 1941 oratorio *A Child of Our Time* made his name as a composer. During World War II he was imprisoned for three months as a conscientious objector. He has written operas, including *King Priam*, symphonies and numerous choral works.

## VAUGHAN WILLIAMS, RALPH (1872-1958) English, born in Down Ampney. After studying at the Royal College of Music, London, Vaughan Williams was later taught by Ravel. He was much influenced by English folk songs. As well as composing symphonies, operas and ballets, he was a conductor and taught at the Royal College of Music.

## VERDI, GIUSEPPE
(1813-1901) Italian, born in Roncole. Verdi's father was a village innkeeper. He studied music with the organist of Bussetto cathedral and in Milan. He then became music

Chiesetta di Roncole

Casa ove nacque G.Verdi a Roncole

NATO IL 10 OTTOBRE 1813

MORTO IL 27 GENNAIO

PROPRIETÀ RISERVATA Stab. F. Collini-Milano

△ *A postcard showing Giuseppe Verdi and his birthplace*

master in Bussetto and began writing operas. Verdi went on to become the most successful opera composer of his generation. The most famous of his 27 operas are *Rigoletto*, *La Traviata*, *Aida* and *Otello*.

## VIVALDI, ANTONIO
(1678-1741) Italian, born in Venice. The son of a professional violinist, Vivaldi trained as a priest but soon became famous as a composer. In 1740 he moved to Vienna, hoping to make a success there, but died a year later in poverty. After his death his work was forgotten until his concertos – particularly *The Four Seasons* – became popular in the 1800s.

## WAGNER, RICHARD
(1813–83) German, born in Leipzig. Wagner became interested in opera at an early age. After studying at Leipzig he held a series of positions in

◁ *Dmitri Shostakovich*

German opera houses and then went to Paris, where he worked on his own opera *The Flying Dutchman*. He returned to Germany as music director of the court of Dresden, but had to leave because of his revolutionary activities. He went to Zurich in Switzerland and began work on a set of four operas called *Der Ring des Nibelungen*. This project took 25 years. By 1865 Wagner was in debt, but was saved by the support of King Ludwig II of Bavaria, who invited him to Munich. Ludwig then provided funds for Wagner to build his own opera house at Bayreuth, and he performed his operas there until his death.

## WALTON, WILLIAM (1902-83) English, born in Oldham. Walton was a chorister at Christchurch College, Oxford.

His first major work was *Façade*, a musical setting for Edith Sitwell's poems. He wrote two symphonies, operas, the oratorio *Belshazzar's Feast*, concertos and chamber music as well as music scores for films.

▽ *Richard Wagner*

# Classical Music

## Facts

The oldest song is the *shaduf* chant sung by workers on the Nile river in Egypt.

The biggest grand piano weighed 1.25 tonnes and was 3.55metres long.

Romanian pianist Cella Delavrancea gave her last public performance at the age of 103.

A record audience of 800,000 attended a free concert by the New York Philharmonic Orchestra conducted by Zubin Mehta, 1986.

The largest choir consisted of 60,000 people and sang at the end of a concert in Breslau, Germany on 2nd August 1937.

The highest price paid at auction for any instrument was £902,000 for a Stradivarius violin in 1990.

In 1991 Placido Domingo was applauded for 1 hour 20 minutes after a performance of *Otello*. Luciano Pavarotti received 165 curtain calls at a concert in Berlin in 1988.

The shortest opera ever is *The Sands of Time* by Simon Rees and Peter Reynolds which at one performance lasted a mere 3 minutes and 34 seconds.

The largest and loudest instrument ever built is the Auditorium Organ in Atlantic City, New Jersey, USA. Now only partly functional, it had the volume of 25 brass bands.

The best-selling classical album is *In Concert* recorded by Carreras, Domingo and Pavarotti. To date it has sold over 5 million copies.

The most spins in a classical ballet is 32 in *Swan Lake*.

The most expensive piano is a Steinway bought for $390,000 in 1980.

## Dates

**BC546** Pythagoras introduces the concept of the musical octave.

**250** First organ invented in Greece.

**AD800** Music becomes widely used in monasteries.

**1025** Guido d'Arezzo's first writings on music. He introduced the idea of giving each joint and fingertip on the hand the name of a note as a way of aiding musical memory.

**1150** Troubadours become very popular in Provence.

**1240** The motet becomes an important form of polyphonic composition.

**1364** One of the first large-scale musical works, Guillaume de Machaut's *Messe de Notre Dame*, is performed at the coronation of Charles V of France in Rheims.

**1473** The earliest known printed music, the *Collectorium Super Magnificat* by Johannes Gerson, is published in Esslingen, Germany.

**c.1550** The violin takes the form and shape we know today.

**1575** English composers Thomas Tallis and William Byrd jointly publish their *Cantiones Sacrae*, a collection of 34 motets, dedicated to Queen Elizabeth I.

**c.1597** The work thought to be the first example of opera, *La Dafne* (or *Dafne*) by Jacopo Peri, is staged privately at the Corsi Palazzo in Florence.

**1610** Monteverdi's *Vespers* is published/composed in Venice.

**1637** World's first opera house opens in Venice.

**1644** Birth of the great violin maker, Antonio Stradivari.

**1709** Bartolommeo Cristofori builds the first pianoforte in Florence.

**1721** Bach composes his *Brandenberg Concertos*, a set of 6 'concerti grossi', dedicated to Christian Ludwig, but apparently never played for him.

**1722** Bach wrote *The Well Tempered Clavier*, a set of preludes and fuges for keyboard in all the major and minor keys, to show off the advantages of the recently introduced system of 'equal temperament'.

**1725** Vivaldi publishes *The Four Seasons*.

**1742** Handel's oratorio *The Messiah* premièred in Dublin.

**755** Haydn writes his first quartets.

**761** Publication of Mozart's *Minuet* and *Trio in G*. He was four years old.

**786** First performance of Mozart's *The Marriage of Figaro*.

**798** Haydn's oratorio *The Creation* first performed in Austria.

**787** Mozart wrote the opera *Don Giovanni*.

**794** Haydn completed his *London Symphonies*.

**795** At the age of 13 the Italian violinist Niccolò Paganini makes his first tour.

**815** As well as various other compositions, Schubert wrote about 144 songs in this year. Maelzel patents the clockwork metronome.

**824** First performance of Beethoven's *Symphony No. 9*.

**835** Tuba invented in Germany.

**846** Adolphe Sax invents the saxophone.

**851** First performance of Verdi's opera *Rigoletto*, in Venice.

**862** Köchel's catalogue of Mozart's works first published.

**1871** Verdi's *Aida* first performed not in Italy but in Cairo. The librettist Gilbert and the composer Sullivan meet and embark on a long collaboration.

**1873** Sir George Grove begins compiling his *Dictionary of Music and Musicians*.

**1875** First performance of Bizet's opera *Carmen*.

**1876** First performance of Wagner's *Ring Cycle* of operas in Bayreuth.

**1877** The phonograph is invented by Edison.

**1885** Gilbert and Sullivan finish *The Mikado*.

**1887** First perfrormance of Verdi's opera *Otello* in Milan.

**1894** The debut of Debussy's *Prélude à l'Apres-midi d'un Faune* caused a scandal because of its supposed 'formlessness'.

**1895** First performance of Puccini's *La Bohème* in Turin.

**1903** First performance of Puccini's *Madame Butterfly* which was a failure. It was revised and re-performed in 1904 and was a huge success.

**1905** First performance of Debussy's orchestral work, *La Mer*.

**1907** First music broadcast.

**1910** Stravinsky finished the music for Diaghilev's ballet *The Firebird*.

**1911** First performance of Strauss' opera *Der Rosenkavalier* in Dresden.

**1913** Stravinsky's *The Rite of Spring* caused a riot at its première in Paris.

**1919** First performance of Holst's *The Planets*

**c.1921** Schoenberg devises twelve-tone system of composition. Earliest examples of this are the *Suite* for piano and the *5 Piano Pieces*.

**1924** First performance of Gershwin's *Rhapsody in Blue*.

**1928** First performance of Ravel's *Bolero* which was originally written as a ballet score.

**1931** Walton's dramatic cantata *Belshazzar's Feast* is first performed at Leeds Festival.

**1935** First performance of Gershwin's *Porgy and Bess* in Boston.

**1936** First performance of Prokofiev's *Peter and the Wolf*.

**1937** First performance of Orff's *Carmina Burana*.

**c.1941** First performance of Copland's *Appalachian Spring*.

**1946** First performance of Prokofiev's *War and Peace* in Leningrad, USSR.

**1949** First performance of Messaien's *Turangalîla Symphony* which uses unusual instruments, such as the ondes martenot.

**1954** First performance of Varèse's *Déserts,* the first work to combine musical instruments and pre-recorded magnetic tape.

**1955** First performance of Boulez's *Le Marteau sans maître*.

**1961** First performance of Britten's *War Requiem*.

**1984** First performance of *Akhnaten* by Glass in Stuttgart.

**1989** First performance of Tippett's opera *New Year*, in London.

**1990** Pavarotti, Domingo and Carreras sing at the World Cup Finals in Rome.

**1992** First performance of Stockhausen's opera *Dienstag aus Licht* in Portugal.

# Musicals

## Facts

*A Chorus Line* holds the record for the longest run on Broadway (New York) with 6,137 performances.

The longest-running musical of all is the off-Broadway show, *The Fantastiks,* which totalled 14,488 performances.

The longest-running musical in London's West End is *Cats.* It passed *A Chorus Line*'s record on 29th January 1996, making it the longest-running major show on either side of the Atlantic.

*Miss Saigon* holds the record for the largest advance sales at the box office at $36m before its 1991 opening on Broadway.

In 1978, Columbia Pictures paid $9.8m for the film rights to the musical *Annie.*

26.5 million copies of the *Saturday Night Fever* (1977) soundtrack were sold up to May 1987, making it the top-selling film soundtrack.

The soundtrack of the film *South Pacific* was No.1 in the first UK album charts in 1958.

## Classic Stage Musicals

**1915** *Very Good, Eddie* – Jerome Kern and Guy Bolton

**1924** *Lady, Be Good* – George and Ira Gershwin

**1927** *Showboat* – Jerome Kern and Oscar Hammerstein II

**1928** *The Threepenny Opera* – Kurt Weill and Bertolt Brecht

**1929** *Mr Cinders* – Vivian Ellis; *Bitter Sweet* – Noel Coward

**1934** *Anything Goes* – Cole Porter

**1935** *Porgy and Bess* – George and Ira Gershwin

**1937** *Me and My Girl* – Noel Gay, Douglas Furber and L Arthur Rose

**1940** *Pal Joey* – Richard Rogers and Lorenz Hart

**1943** *Oklahoma!* – Richard Rogers and Oscar Hammerstein II

**1956** *My Fair Lady* – Fritz Loewe and Alan Jay Lerner

**1957** *West Side Story* – Leonard Bernstein and Stephen Sondheim

**1960** *Oliver!* – Lionel Bart; *The Fantastiks* – Harvey Schmidt and Tom Jones

**1964** *Fiddler on the Roof* – Jerry Beck and Sheldon Harnick

**1966** *Cabaret* – John Kander and Fred Ebb

**1968** *Hair* – Galt MacDermot, James Rado and Gerome Rgni

**1972** *Jesus Christ, Superstar* – Andrew Lloyd Webber and Tim Rice

**1973** *A Little Night Music* – Stephen Sondheim

**1975** *A Chorus Line* – Marvin Hamlisch and Edward Kleban

**1978** *Evita* – Andrew Lloyd Webber and Tim Rice

**1984** *Sunday in the Park with George* – Stephen Sondheim

**1985** *Les Miserables* – Claude-Michel Schönberg and Alain Boublil

**1986** *The Phantom of the Opera* – Andrew Lloyd Webber and Charles Hart

**1993** *Sunset Boulevard* – Andrew Lloyd Webber and Don Black

## Classic Musicals Conceived as Movies

**1929** *Broadway Melody* – Nacio Herb Brown and Arthur Freed

**1933** *42nd Street* – Harry Warren and Al Dubin

**1935** *Top Hat* – Irving Berlin

**1937** *Shall We Dance?* – George and Ira Gershwin

**1939** *The Wizard of Oz* – Harold Arlen and Yip Harburg

**1944** *Meet Me in St Louis* – Hugh Martin and Ralph Blame

**1948** *Easter Parade* – Irving Berlin

**1951** *An American In Paris* – Nacio Herb Brown and Arthur Freed

**1952** *Singin' in the Rain* – Nacio Herb Brown and Arthur Freed

**1953** *The Band Wagon* – Arthur Schwartz and Howard Dietz

**1954** *A Star is Born* – Harold Arlen and Ira Gershwin

**1958** *Gigi* – Fritz Loewe and Alan Jay Lerner; *King Creole* – Jerry Lieber and Mike Stoller

# Jazz

## Jazz Terms

**Bebop** A name used to describe the jazz of Charlie Parker and others, but originally meaning 'Go, man, go!' in African-American slang.

**Combo** Abbreviation of combination. A group of musicians.

**Dixieland** Often used to describe New Orleans jazz, the term may derive from the French word 'dix' meaning ten and a $10 bill was printed in New Orleans.

**Horn** Jazz term for any brass or woodwind instrument.

**Jam-session** An informal gathering of musicians playing jazz for their own enjoyment.

**Riff** A repeated, brief, distinctive musical phrase.

**Syncopation** One of the key attributes of jazz, it involves accenting normally unstressed beats in a musical bar.

## Classic Jazz Recordings

**1916** *Scott Joplin*

**1923** *Canal Street Blues* – King Oliver's Jazz Band

**1924-28** *The Bix Beiderbecke Legend* – Bix Beiderbecke

**1925-27** *The Bessie Smith Story Vol 3* – Bessie Smith

**1926-28** *The King of New Orleans Jazz* – Jelly Roll Morton

**1928** *Louis Armstrong and Earl Hines* – Louis Armstrong and Earl Hines

**1930** *Mood Indigo* – Duke Ellington

**1937-38** *The Golden Years Vol 2* – Billie Holiday

**1938** *The Carnegie Hall Concert* – Benny Goodman

**1939** *Undecided* – Ella Fitzgerald

**1946-47** *Bird Lives* – Charlie Parker; *Sassy Sings* – Sarah Vaughan

**1947** *Genius of Modern Music* – Thelonius Monk

**1949-50** *Birth of the Cool* – Miles Davis

**1954** *A Night at Birdland* – Art Blakey

**1956** *Saxophone Colossus* – Sonny Rollins

**1957** *The Hawk Flies High* – Coleman Hawkins

**1958** *Somethin' Else* – Cannonball Adderley; *The Sermon* – Jimmy Smith

**1959** *Time Out* – Dave Brubeck; *The Shape of Jazz to Come* – Ornette Coleman; *Kind of Blue* – Miles Davis

**1960** *My Favourite Things* – John Coltrane

**1963** *The Black Saint and the Sinner Lady* – Charles Mingus; *Our Man in Paris* – Dexter Gordon; *Night Train* – Oscar Peterson

**1964** *The Sidewinder* – Lee Morgan

**1969** *Bitches' Brew* – Miles Davis

**1972** *Head Hunter* – Herbie Hancock

**1975** *Native Dancer* – Wayne Shorter

**1977** *Heavy Weather* – Weather Report

**1982** *Bobby McFerrin* – Bobby McFerrin

**1985** *Song X* – Pat Metheny

**1986** *Standard Time* – Wynton Marsalis; *On the Edge of Tomorrow* – Steve Coleman

**1991** *The Language of Truth* – Julian Joseph

**1992** *To the Eyes of Creation* – Courtney Pine

# Rock and Pop

## Facts

Between 300,000 and 500,000 people attended the first of the giant pop festivals, the Woodstock Music and Art Fair in Bethel, New York from 15th to 17th August, 1969.

The estimated 3.5 million people who saw Rod Stewart play a free concert in Rio de Janeiro, on New Year's Eve 1988, are thought to be the biggest rock audience ever.

Michael Jackson played to 504,000 people on seven sell-out nights at Wembley Stadium, London in July and August 1988.

The Rolling Stones have won the most gold records for a group – 39. Chicago won the most platinum records with 17. Paul McCartney has won 13 platinum discs, the most for any male performer.

Stevie Wonder, with 17 awards, is the top Grammy Award winner.

Elvis Presley's estate was presented with 50 platinum and 60 gold discs, a world record.

Michael Jackson won a record 8 Grammy Awards in 1984.

'Rock Around the Clock', released in 1954 by Bill Haley and his Comets, is estimated to have sold the most copies of any single at 25 million.

Michael Jackson's *Thriller* (1982) is the best-selling album of all time with worldwide sales of over 47 million copies.

Fleetwood Mac's *Rumours* (1970) has sold 21 million copies, making it the best-selling album by any group.

The best-selling album in the UK is The Beatles' *Sgt. Pepper's Lonely Hearts Club Band* (1967).

The Beatles' 'Can't Buy Me Love' (1964) had the greatest advance sales of any single with 2.2 million copies ordered worldwide.

*Bat Out of Hell* (1979) by Meat Loaf totalled the most weeks on the UK album chart with 471 up to April 1994.

Pink Floyd's *Dark Side of the Moon* (1973) spent a record 741 weeks in the US album charts up to the end of 1992.

'My Way' (1969) by Frank Sinatra totalled the most weeks spent on the UK singles chart with 77.

'Tainted Love' (1987) by Soft Cell spent a record 43 weeks in a row on the US Billboard Hot 100.

The Beatles hold the record for the most consecutive UK No.1 singles with 11.

The Beatles had a record 20 No.1 US singles.

Bryan Adams' '(Everything I Do) I Do for You' (1992) spent a record 16 consecutive weeks at No.1 in the UK singles chart.

Whitney Houston's 'I Will Always Love You' (1992) and Boyz II Men's 'I'll Make Love to You' (1994) hold the record jointly for the longest stay at No.1 in the US singles chart with 14 weeks.

Cliff Richard holds the record for the most UK hit singles, with 115 up to December 1994.

Elvis Presley had a record 149 releases on the US Billboard singles chart up to 1990.

The Beatles had a record 15 No.1 albums in the US charts. Elvis Presley had the most hit US albums with 92.

In 1991 Michael Jackson signed a $890m recording contract with Sony – believed to be the largest music contract in history.

## Classic Releases

### Singles

**1955** 'Rock around the Clock' – Bill Haley and the Comets

**1956** 'Heartbreak Hotel' – Elvis Presley

**1958** 'All I Have to do is Dream' – The Everly Brothers

**1959** 'It Doesn't Matter Any More' – Buddy Holly

**1960** 'Three Steps to Heaven' – Eddie Cochran

**1963** 'I Want to Hold Your Hand' – The Beatles

**1964** 'Pretty Woman' – Roy Orbison

**1965** 'Satisfaction' – The Rolling Stones

**1966** 'River Deep and Mountain High' – Ike and Tina Turner

**1967** 'All You Need is Love' – The Beatles

**1968** 'Sitting on the Dock of the Bay' – Otis Redding

**1969** 'I Heard It Through the Grapevine' – Marvin Gaye

**1971** 'Hot Love' – T Rex

**1972** 'School's Out' – Alice Cooper

**1975** 'Bohemian Rhapsody' – Queen

**1976** 'Anarchy in the UK' – The Sex Pistols

**1979** 'Sunday Girl' – Blondie

**1981** 'Tainted Love' – Soft Cell

**1983** 'Billie Jean' – Michael Jackson

**1984** 'Do They Know it's Christmas?' – Band Aid

**1985** 'Into the Groove' – Madonna

**1987** 'It's A Sin' – The Pet Shop Boys

**1990** 'Ice Ice Baby' – Vanilla Ice

**1991** '(Everything I Do) I Do For You' – Bryan Adams

**1992** 'I Will Always Love You' – Whitney Houston

**1993** 'I'll Do Anything For Love (But I Won't Do That)' – Meat Loaf

**1994** 'Love Is All Around' – Wet Wet Wet

### Albums

**1963** *With the Beatles* – The Beatles

**1964** *Bringing It All Back Home* – Bob Dylan

**1965** *Aftermath* – The Rolling Stones

**1966** *Revolver* – The Beatles

**1967** *Sgt. Pepper's Lonely Hearts Club Band* – The Beatles

**1968** *Electric Ladyland* – Jimi Hendrix

**1969** *Tommy* – The Who

**1970** *Bridge Over Troubled Water* – Simon and Garfunkel

**1971** *Imagine* – John Lennon

**1972** *Ziggy Stardust* – David Bowie

**1973** *Tubular Bells* – Mike Oldfield

**1974** *Queen 2* – Queen

**1975** *Blood on the Tracks* – Bob Dylan

**1976** *Hotel California* – The Eagles

**1977** *Rumours* – Fleetwood Mac

**1978** *This Year's Model* – Elvis Costello

**1979** *Bat Out of Hell* – Meat Loaf

**1980** *Hotter Than July* – Stevie Wonder

**1982** *Thriller* – Michael Jackson

**1983** *Swordfishtrombones* – Tom Waits

**1984** *Born in the USA* – Bruce Springsteen

**1985** *Brothers in Arms* – Dire Straits

**1986** *Graceland* – Paul Simon

**1987** *Tunnel of Love* – Bruce Springsteen

**1988** *Naked* – Talking Heads

**1989** *New York* – Lou Reed

**1990** *Immaculate Collection* – Madonna

**1991** *Stars* – Simply Red

**1992** *Automatic for the People* – REM

**1993** *Home Invasion* – Ice-T

**1994** *Park Life* – Blur

**1995** *What's the Story, Morning Glory* – Oasis

WOODSTOCK

The Who

Janis Joplin

Jimi Hendrix

Joan Baez

Crosby, Stills, Nash and Young

Santana

John Sebastian

Ravi Shankar

Jefferson Airplane

Keef Hartley Band

# Glossary

**Absolute music** Instrumental music composed purely as music, without aiming to tell a story or interpret a work of art. The opposite of programme music.

**Accidental** A sign, such as a sharp, flat or natural, which is used in music notation to alter the pitch of a note. An accidental not only affects the note which follows it, but also any other notes of the same pitch which appear later in the bar. After a bar-line, the notes return to their normal pitch.

**Accompaniment** The musical background that supports the main part in a piece of music. For example, a singer might perform songs 'with piano accompaniment'.

**Acoustics** The science of sound and how it is produced. *Also,* the characteristics of a building (e.g. shape, size), which affect how sound is heard. For example, a concert hall will be designed to have good acoustics so that the audience will be able to hear clearly and without distortion.

**Aerophone** A musical instrument that uses vibrating air to produce a sound. Most aerophones are blown by the performer (e.g. flute, trumpet, bagpipe), but some use a mechanical device to make air vibrate (e.g. organ).

**Aleatory music** A type of music in which some parts of the composition or performance are left to chance. For example, this might mean asking the performer to throw dice to decide which section to play next, interpret a graphic score or improvise.

**Anthem** A short piece for choir on a religious theme. An anthem is similar to a motet, but is used in the Protestant not the Roman Catholic church and sung in English instead of Latin. *Also,* a hymn-like song that is used for special occasions. For example, the National Anthem.

**Antiphony** The effect created when two groups of musicians, positioned some distance apart, perform alternately so that one group seems to be 'answering' the other.

**Aria** A vocal piece, generally for just one singer, with instrumental accompaniment. Arias are usually found in large compositions such as operas.

▽ *Bagpipes*

**Arpeggio** A chord in which the notes are played one after the other instead of all at the same time. Sometimes notes are played from top to bottom, but usually from bottom to top.

**Arrangement** A piece of music that has been adapted so that it can be played by instruments other than those the composer intended. For example, a composition for orchestra might be 'arranged' so that it could be played on the piano.

**Atonal music** Music that has no key. Atonal music treats all twelve notes of the chromatic scale equally.

**Ballet** A form of entertainment in which performers dance and mime to music. The dancers interpret the music using a variety of movements and expressions to create moods and tell stories.

**Bar** A small section of a piece of music. Music is split up into bars by vertical lines known as bar-lines, and each bar contains the number of beats shown in the time signature. A double bar-line (a thin line followed by a thick one) is used at the end of a piece.

**Baroque music** Music that was composed during the period 1600 to 1750. Composers such as Johann Sebastian Bach, Antonio Vivaldi, Archangelo Corelli and George Frideric Handel wrote during this period. *Also,* used to describe art and architecture. Many different musical forms became important at this time, including the opera, oratorio, sonata and dance suite.

**Beat** A unit of time used in music. In each bar, notes are grouped together in beats to make them easier to read. For example, in 3/4 the notes are grouped in three crotchet beats. In 6/8 they are grouped in two dotted crotchet beats.

**Blues** A kind of folk music that first became popular in the USA in the 1860s. It was based on spiritual and work songs, and is usually rather sad and slow. The blues often uses a twelve-bar chord sequence and special 'blue notes' (flattened notes) to create its distinctive sound. It has influenced many other types of music, especially jazz.

**Cadence** The end of a phrase or section of a piece of music. A cadence is generally made up of two chords, played one after the other. Sometimes the chords make the music sound complete and finished ('perfect cadence'), but sometimes they sound incomplete ('imperfect cadence') or unexpected ('interrupted cadence').

**Cadenza** A section in a composition for a solo performer where the accompaniment stops playing and the soloist has the opportunity to show off their technique. Cadenzas are most often found in concertos. In some cases they are written by the composer and in others they are left for the performer to improvise.

**Canon** A piece made up of different parts that copy one another. Each part uses exactly the same notes, but they start at different times, each new one joining a short time after the last. A simple form of canon is called a round.

**Carol** A type of song used to celebrate many different occasions such as religious festivals and the changing of the seasons. Today, the word 'carol' is generally used to describe a song or hymn that is sung at Christmas time.

**Chamber music** Music performed by a small group of people, rather than by a soloist or an orchestra. For example, a string quartet or a piano trio.

**Chord** Any two or more notes that are played at the same time. Chords create harmony in music and make it sound complete.

**Chordophone** A musical instrument that produces a sound when a string is made to vibrate, by plucking (e.g. guitar, harp), hitting (e.g. piano) or bowing (e.g. violin, cello).

▷ *A cello (chordophone)*

**Chorus** A group of singers in a vocal composition. Unlike soloists, the chorus all sing together, either in unison, or in smaller groups with several voices to each part. *Also,* the part of a song that is repeated between verses, sometimes also called the 'refrain'.

**Chromatic scale** A musical scale that is made up of twelve notes, each a semitone apart. For example, on the piano you can find a chromatic scale by playing from any one note to the next one with the same letter name, using all the black and white notes in between.

**Classical music** In the strictest sense, music mainly composed during the period from 1750 to 1830, by composers such as Joseph Haydn, Wolfgang Amadeus Mozart and Ludwig van Beethoven. During this time, many of the musical forms used today became very important – for example, the symphony, the concerto and the string quartet. However, in general the word now means music that is more permanent than popular or light music.

**Clef** A sign that is placed at the beginning of each line of a piece of music. By looking at the clef it is possible to work out the exact pitch of all the notes on and around the stave. There are four different types of clef – treble, alto, tenor and bass.

**Coda** A final section of a piece, carefully composed to make the music sound as though it has come to an end.

**Concerto** A piece for one or more solo instruments and orchestra, usually in three movements. Concertos are popular as showpieces because they give the performer(s) plenty of opportunity to display their virtuosity and technique – particularly in the cadenzas.

**Concert pitch** Musicians tune instruments to concert pitch so that when they play together they are in tune. It is internationally agreed that at concert pitch the A above

*The note Middle C written using the four types of clef.*

Middle C has a frequency of 440 hertz. That means it is made up of 440 vibrations per second.

**Conductor** The person who directs a group of instrumentalists or singers such as an orchestra or a choir. Conducting not only involves keeping a steady beat and making sure that everyone plays or sings at the right time, but also interpreting the music. It is the conductor's job to decide on tempo, dynamics and phrasing, as well as to check that there is a good balance of sound, with no one part sounding too loud or too quiet.

△ *A conductor*

**Continuo** A kind of accompaniment often used in Baroque music. The continuo part was generally played by a combination of instruments such as cello and harpsichord, with one playing the bass line and the other improvising harmonies around it.

**Counterpoint** The combination of two or more independent lines of music. In 'contrapuntal' music (music that uses counterpoint), there are often many different melodic lines all playing at the same time – not just one playing the tune and others accompanying it. Similar to polyphony.

**Descant** The part sung by the highest voices in a piece of choral music. *Also,* a high counter-melody (a melody that is not the main tune), sung by sopranos or trebles in a well-known song such as a hymn.

**Duet** A piece for two instruments or voices, either with or without accompaniment.

**Duple time** Music that has two beats in each bar for example, 2/4 (below) or 6/8.

**Dynamics** The different levels of volume used in music. Dynamic markings tell the performer how loudly or quietly to play and when to change from one volume to another. The most commonly used dynamic markings are *fortissimo* (***ff***) = very loud
*forte* (***f***) = loud
*crescendo* = get gradually louder
*mezzo forte* (***mf***) = quite loud
*diminuendo* = get gradually quieter
*piano* (***p***) = quiet

*mezzo piano* (**mp**) = quite quiet
*pianissimo* (or **pp**) = very quiet

**Electrophone** A musical instrument that produces sound electronically, such as a synthesizer.

**Encore** A French word that means 'again'. At the end of

a concert, the audience may shout 'Encore!' as a way of asking the performer to play some more, perhaps to repeat something they have already played, or to play something completely different. The piece that is played as a result is also known as an encore.

**Fingering** The technique of using the fingers to produce a note from a musical instrument. Small numbers are sometimes printed above or below notes to help musicians work out which fingers to use, especially in music for keyboard instruments such as the piano.

**Flat** A sign that lowers the pitch of the note that follows it by a semitone. It also affects all other notes of the same pitch that appear later in the same bar. *Also,* a word that describes a musical sound or performance which is lower in pitch than it should be e.g. 'Her singing was flat'.

**Folk music** Tunes and songs that are passed on from one generation of people to the next, sometimes without ever being written down. Folk songs were generally found among country-dwellers, and spread to cities during the 1700s to 1800s. Some of the

most common types of folk music are children's songs, dance tunes and songs that are used in rituals and religious ceremonies. Many composers have made use of folk music in their compositions from Renaissance times to Joseph Haydn, Edvard Grieg, Pyotr Tchaikovsky, Ralph Vaughan Williams and Béla Bartók.

**Fret** A strip of wood, metal or gut that runs across the fingerboard of a stringed instrument such as a guitar, lute or *sitar*. The violin has no frets. Frets are used to show the player where the fingers need to be placed in order to produce particular notes.

**Fugue** A type of contrapuntal piece (see counterpoint) in which musical ideas are first played by one part, then imitated by others, with each one joining in a short while after the last.

**Fundamental** The name for the lowest harmonic.

**Gagaku** A Japanese word meaning graceful or elegant music, and used to describe an art form involving both music and dancing.

**Gamelan** A type of orchestra found in South East Asia, particularly on the islands of Java and Bali (now Indonesia). Although there are many different kinds of *gamelan*, they all include percussion instruments such as gongs, metallophones and drums. Some also include flutes and stringed instruments.

**Graphic score** A score that uses pictures and symbols instead of ordinary musical notation. The performer is asked to create the music by looking at the score and imagining the kind of sounds, dynamics and moods the signs represent.

**Harmonics** Each musical sound is made up of lots of different vibrations. For example, when a string vibrates, it not only vibrates as a whole, but also in halves, thirds, quarters and so on. Each kind of vibration produces a different pitch, known as a harmonic. However, it is usually only possible to hear the lowest, loudest harmonic (in this case, the sound of the whole string vibrating) – this is called the fundamental.

**Harmony** The sounding of different notes at the same time to form chords. The movement from one chord to another is known as a harmonic progression. Along with melody and rhythm, harmony is one of the most important elements used in music.

**Hymn** A religious song. Hymns have been used for many centuries in the Christian church as a way of singing praise to God.

**Idiophone** A musical instrument that produces a sound when it is hit, scraped or rubbed. In an idiophone, the sound is made by the vibration of the instrument itself (e.g. gong, triangle), not by a separate string as in a violin (chordophone), or skin as in a drum (membranophone).

**Improvisation** The process of making up music as you go along, without playing from a musical score or from memory. It is often used in pieces where some of the decisions are left to the performer – for example, in the cadenzas of a concerto, or in compositions that use unusual notation. It is also an important feature of jazz.

**Interval** The distance in pitch between any two notes. This is measured by counting up the notes of the scale from one to the other. For example, the distance from C to G is five notes, C-D-E-F-G. This interval between C and G is called a fifth.

**Intonation** The tuning of a musician's performance. If someone has 'good intonation', it means that they are in tune, if they have 'bad intonation' they are out of tune.

**Jazz** A type of popular music that appeared in the USA around 1890. It had many influences including the blues, traditional African rhythms, ragtime, work songs, gospel singing and the music that was popular in Europe at the time.

*A jazz band*

Jazz often uses syncopated rhythms and improvisation around a melody line or a chord sequence. There are many different kinds, including New Orleans style, Dixieland, swing, bebop, cool, fusion and free-form.

**Jongleur** During the Middle Ages, a jongleur was a professional entertainer who travelled from place to place. As well as singing and playing an instrument, a jongleur would probably also have been a skilled acrobat or juggler. Similar to a minstrel.

**Kettledrum** Tuned percussion instrument with a single skin stretched over a pot or vessel body. In the orchestra, kettledrums are often known as timpani.

**Key** The scale around which a piece of music is based. A piece that mainly uses the notes of the scale of C major, is said to be 'in the key of C major'. The first note of the scale, which gives it its name, is called the 'keynote'. *Also,* a lever on an instrument, such as a piano or flute, which is pressed down to produce a note.

**Keyboard** The arrangement of levers or keys on an instrument such as a piano or organ.

**Key signature** A sign that is written after the clef at the beginning of each line of a piece of music. It is usually made up of one or more sharps or flats which show the performer which key the music is in, and which notes need to be sharpened or flattened when playing it.

**Koto** A Japanese long-necked zither, with 13 silk strings stretched over adjustable bridges.

**Ledger/leger lines** Short lines that are added above or below the staff when writing notes that are too high or low to fit on the staff itself.

**Legato** An instruction to play smoothly, without pausing between notes.

**Libretto** The words of a piece of music such as an opera, oratorio or cantata.

**Lieder** A German word meaning 'song'. It is generally used to describe a type of vocal composition that was popular with German and Austrian composers during the Romantic period of the 1800s. Lieder are songs for solo voice and piano, with the piano part sometimes acting as an accompaniment to the vocal line, and sometimes as an equal partner.

**Madrigal** A kind of vocal composition, generally for several voices without accompaniment. Madrigals were first sung in Italy towards the end of the 1200s, and became especially popular in the 1500s. Unlike motets and anthems, the words in madrigals were not based on religious texts, but on poems about love and country life.

**Major scale** One of the most commonly used scales in Western music, the major scale is always made up of the same pattern of intervals. The distance between each pair of notes in the scale is a tone – apart from notes three and four and notes seven and eight, which are both a semitone apart. To find the scale of C major on a piano keyboard, simply play from one C to the next, using only the white notes.

**Mass** A large composition for choir which is based on the main service of the Roman Catholic church. Sometimes there is also instrumental accompaniment and solo singers.

**Melody** A series of notes (of varying pitch) that is played one after the other to form a musical line, or tune. Along with harmony and rhythm, melody is one of the most important elements used in music.

**Membranophone** A musical instrument that produces a sound when a stretched 'membrane' or skin is made to vibrate. Many kinds of drum are known as membranophones. They are usually struck by the hand or a beater.

*Tsuzumi drum*

**Middle C** The C that is nearest to the middle of the piano keyboard.

**MIDI** A word that stands for '*M*usical *I*nstrument *D*igital *I*nterface'. Most pieces of electronic musical equipment such as keyboards, synthesizers and samplers use MIDI to communicate with one another. Instruments or computers that use MIDI are said to be 'MIDI compatible'.

**Minor scale** A type of scale that has two different forms, the harmonic minor and the melodic minor. As the names suggest, the notes of the harmonic minor scale are mainly used in the harmonies of a piece of music, and the notes of the melodic scale are used in the melody line or tune. The melodic minor scale is unusual, because it uses one set of notes to go up the scale and another to come down again. However, there is one important feature which is common to both types of scale, the third note (or 'degree') of any minor scale is a semitone lower than in a major scale beginning on the same note. (Here is a picture of part of the G melodic minor scale)

**Minstrel** A professional musician and entertainer who lived during the Middle Ages – particularly one who could play at least one sort of musical instrument. Like jongleurs, minstrels sometimes worked with other performers such as troubadours, accompanying their songs on the lute.

**Minuet** A type of French dance in triple time. It was originally popular with composers of dance music during the Baroque period. Later, Classical composers such as Wolfgang Amadeus Mozart began to use it too, often as a movement of a work such as a symphony or string quartet.

**Modes** One of the scales on which most Western music was based until the end of the 1500s. Modes have traditionally been used in forms of church music such as plainsong, and sometimes also in folk music. Two of the modes, the Ionian (the white notes from C to C on a piano) and the Aeolian (the white notes from A to A) were adapted to become the major and minor scales we know today.

**Monophony** A word meaning 'single sound', used to describe music made up of a single melodic line with no accompaniment.

**Motet** A short choral piece, generally with words based on the Latin texts used in the Roman Catholic church. Motets are often sung unaccompanied. Similar to an anthem.

**Movement** One of the separate sections found in a composition such as a symphony, string quartet, concerto or sonata. Pieces often contain several different movements, each one in a slightly different mood or tempo. For example, there are often four movements in a symphony, three in a concerto and so on.

**Natural** A sign that is used during a piece of music to cancel a flat or a sharp sign that appears either earlier in the same bar, or in the key signature. Like other accidentals, a natural affects all other notes of the same pitch that follow it in a bar. Also the name for a note that is not sharpened or flattened. For example, the note C can also be called C natural.

**Notation** A way of writing music down. There are many different types of musical notation used around the world, but the Western system of writing notes on the lines and spaces of a staff is one of the most popular.

**Note** A musical sound, or the sign used to write it down.

**Note values**
*Crotchet* A note that lasts for one count. Also called a 'quarter note'.
*Minim* A note that lasts for two counts. Also called a 'half note'.
*Quaver* A note that lasts for half a count. Also called an 'eighth note'.
*Semibreve* A note that lasts for four counts. Also called a 'whole note'.
*Semiquaver* A note that lasts for a quarter of a count. Also called a 'sixteenth note'.

*Crotchet*

*Minim*

*Quaver*

*Semibreve*

Semiquaver

**Octave** An interval of eight notes. This is the distance between any note and the note immediately above or below it that shares the same letter name.

**Open string** A string on an instrument such as a violin that is not 'stopped' or pressed down by the fingers.

**Opera** A dramatic work in which a story is told through singing and acting. Like a play, an opera is performed on a stage (generally in an opera house or theatre), with

lighting and special costumes for the cast. An orchestra usually performs an overture at the beginning of the opera, and also accompanies the singers in arias and choruses.

**Opus** A word meaning work, which is used by composers when keeping records of their compositions. Each piece of music is given an opus number when it is composed or published for the first time, for example 'Op. 28'. When pieces are composed as a group, they usually share opus numbers, for example 'Op. 101 No. 1', 'Op. 102 No. 2' and so on.

**Oratorio** A composition, usually based on a religious story, which is performed by vocal soloists, chorus and orchestra. The earliest oratorios were acted out in theatres and used special costumes and scenery. This is no longer the case – oratorios are performed in concert halls and churches.

**Orchestra** A mixed group of instruments, including a large number of strings and often wind and percussion as well. The most common type of orchestra is the symphony orchestra, which is made up of four different sections – strings, woodwind, brass and percussion. There are also other types, such as the chamber orchestra (a small version of the symphony orchestra), string orchestra (string instruments only), and theatre orchestra (used in theatres to accompany musicals or ballets).

**Organum** An early form of polyphonic music based on the melodies used in plainsong, which was first used in the AD800s.

**Overture** An instrumental composition used to introduce

a dramatic work such as an opera or an oratorio, though sometimes also performed as a concert piece on its own.

**Part** The music used by each of the different groups of performers in a musical ensemble. For example, in orchestral music, the 'cello part' is the name for the music played by the cellos.

**Pedal** A lever on a musical instrument that is pressed by the foot. Sometimes pedals are used as a way of playing notes (e.g. organ), sustaining them, making them sound quieter (e.g. piano) or changing their pitch (e.g. kettledrum or harp). *Also,* a word used in harmony to describe a note that is held or played repeatedly while the melody and harmonies of the piece change around it.

**Phrase** A group of notes that make up a section of a melody. 'Phrase marks' – curved lines above or below the staff – are sometimes used to show which notes or bars make up each phrase.

**Pitch** How high or low a musical sound is. Each sound is made up of vibrations. The number of vibrations per second is known as the 'frequency'. A note that is high in pitch will vibrate more quickly and have a higher frequency than a low-pitched one.

**Plainsong** A form of vocal music based on the religious texts traditionally used in the Roman Catholic church. The melodies are based around special scales known as 'modes', and they are usually sung unaccompanied, either by soloists, or by a choir singing in unison. 'Gregorian chant' is one of the most famous forms of this type of music.

**Polyphony** A word meaning 'many sounds', used to describe music that combines at least two independent melodic lines. Another word with a similar meaning is 'counterpoint'.

**Pop music** Originally a style of music that appeared during the 1950s in the USA. Today, pop music is a general term used to describe many different kinds of popular, non-classical music including rock, reggae, dance and soul. Songs are the most common form of pop music.

**Programme music** Music inspired by literature, art or nature, and used to tell a story or make the listener imagine pictures or places. The opposite of absolute music.

**Punk rock** A kind of rock music that combines simple tunes and harmonies with words about rebellion against authority. It became popular in Britain and the USA during the 1970s, as a result of bands like the Sex Pistols.

**Quadruple time** Music that has four beats in each bar for example, 4/4 or 12/8.

**Quartet** The word used to describe a composition for four voices or instruments, or the group of people who perform it. For example, the words 'string quartet' can either describe a piece of chamber music written for two violins, viola and cello, or the four musicians who play this type of piece. There are notable quartets by most of the great composers.

**Raga** One of the many patterns of notes on which pieces of Indian classical music are based. The notes of each raga are specially chosen to conjure up a particular mood or emotion for example,

bravery or love, and different *ragas* are played according to the time of day or season.

**Ragtime** A type of dance music, usually composed for solo piano, that became popular in the USA at the end of the 1800s. A rag, or a ragtime piece, was generally in 2/4 or 4/4 time, with a march-like bass line played by the left hand, while the right hand played a syncopated melody over the top. The most famous piano rags were written by Scott Joplin, composer of the 'Maple Leaf Rag' and 'The Entertainer'.

**Rap** A kind of pop music that first appeared during the 1970s in New York. In rap music, words are spoken rhythmically rather than being sung to a tune.

**Reed** A piece of cane or metal that vibrates when air passes across it, used to produce a sound in reed instruments such as the saxophone, accordion and

*Oboe    Clarinet*

organ. Apart from the flute, all the woodwind instruments of the orchestra use reeds. Some use one (e.g. clarinet) and some two (e.g. oboe).

**Refrain** The part of a song that is repeated at the end of each verse or section. In popular music of the 1900s the word 'chorus' has the same meaning.

**Reggae** A kind of popular Jamaican music that first appeared during the 1960s, and since then has influenced pop music around the world. Reggae music is in quadruple time (generally 4/4), with a strong accent on the second and fourth beats of each bar.

**Register** The range of the human voice is split into paths known as registers. Each one is associated with a different area of the body, and has its own distinctive sound. For example, the low register is sometimes known as the chest voice because low notes seem to resonate in the chest of the singer. The high register is also called the head voice because high notes seem to resonate in the head of the singer and so on.

*Pitch range of the tenor voice*

**Requiem** A mass which is sung in remembrance of people who have died. 'Requiem' is a Latin word meaning 'rest'.

**Rest** A silence in music, or the sign used to represent it. There are many different types of rest for example, a crotchet rest which lasts for one crotchet beat, a quaver rest which lasts for one quaver beat and so on.

**Rhythm** The pattern of long and short notes in a piece of music – also, the number of beats in each bar, the use of accented notes and so on. Rhythm has nothing to do with tempo. However quickly or slowly a piece is played, the rhythm stays the same. Along with melody and harmony, rhythm is one of the most important elements used in music.

**Rock music** A type of pop music with strong rhythms and a heavy beat, that was known as 'rock and roll' when it first became popular in the USA in the 1950s. Rock music is usually performed by groups which include a lead singer, amplified guitars and drums.

**Romantic music** Mainly composed between 1830 to 1900, Romantic music was freer and more emotional than the music of the Classical and Baroque periods. Among the forms which became popular at this time were *lieder* and the tone poem (a type of orchestral programme music). Many famous operas, symphonies and concertos were also written in this period, by composers such as Johannes Brahms and Richard Wagner.

**Scale** A series of notes played one after the other, either from the lowest note to the highest (an ascending scale) or from the highest note to the lowest (a descending scale). There are many different types for example, major, minor and chromatic scales.

*Scale of C major*

**Scherzo** An Italian word meaning jest or joke. A lively and often humorous piece in triple time. Generally the *scherzo* is used as the 2nd or 3rd movement of a work such as a sonata, string quartet or symphony. Ludwig van Beethoven wrote many memorable *scherzi*.

**Score** A copy of a piece of music in which all the different instruments' parts are shown. A conductor will use a score to look at all the parts at the same time.

# GLOSSARY

**Semitone** Half a tone. The smallest interval between any two notes on a keyboard.

**Serial music** Music composed using a twelve-note technique known as serialism. A composer of serial music might not only use a series of notes as the basis for a piece, but also a series of note lengths or dynamics. Sometimes, all the different elements of the music are controlled in this way for example, tone quality attack. This is known as total serialism.

**Sforzando** An instruction to make a note sound 'forced' or emphasized. Another word with the same meaning is *sforzato*. Both words can be shortened to *sf* or *sfz* when they are written on a piece of music.

**Sharp** A sign that raises the pitch of the note which follows it by a semitone. The sign also affects all the other notes of the same pitch which appear later in the same bar. *Also,* a word that describes a musical sound or performance which is higher in pitch than it should be.

**Solo** A piece (or section of a piece) composed for a single voice or instrument, either with or without accompaniment.

**Sonata** One of the most important forms of instrumental music from the Baroque period until the present day. A sonata often has three or four contrasting movements, and is generally composed either for a solo instrument, or for one or more other instruments usually with piano accompaniment. For example, a flute sonata is a sonata for flute and piano and so on.

**Song** A short composition for solo voice, either with or without accompaniment. The song is one of the oldest and most popular musical forms, and features in the musical traditions of all peoples.

**Staccato** An Italian word that means 'detached'. Staccato notes (usually shown by a small dot above the head of each one) should be played slightly shorter than usual.

**Staff/stave** A set of five parallel lines used in musical notation. Notes are placed on and around the lines of the staff, and a clef is added at the beginning to show the exact pitch of each note.

**Stop** A handle or switch on an organ that is used to control the flow of air into the pipes and, as a result, the sound the organ makes.

**Swing** A form of jazz that was very popular during the 1930s and 1940s. Swing was often played by 'big bands' for example, the bands of Duke Ellington, Count Basie and Benny Goodman, and people not only enjoyed listening to Swing but dancing to it as well.

**Symphony** One of the most popular and important forms of instrumental music since the Classical period. Symphonies are composed for orchestra, and usually includes four contrasting movements, each one with a slightly different mood or tempo. Because the symphony often uses a similar structure to a sonata, it is sometimes described as a kind of 'sonata for orchestra'.

**Syncopation** An effect created when an accent is placed on a note that would not normally be accented. Each bar of music is made up of strong and weak beats – for example, in 4/4, beats one and three are stronger than beats two and four. When a note on a weak beat is accented and made to sound more important than a note on a strong beat, the rhythm is said to be syncopated. Syncopation is found in many different types of music, particularly in the rhythms of traditional African music and jazz.

**Tempo** The speed of a piece of music. Traditionally, composers have used tempo markings to describe the speed of their music, but these only give the performer a rough idea. A more exact way of describing tempo is to use a metronome mark. For example, M.M. ♩ = 60 tells you that the piece should be played at a speed of 60 crotchet beats per minute. M.M. ♩ = 100 means there are 100 minim beats in a minute. M.M. stands for Maelzels's metronome.

## Tempo markings

| | |
|---|---|
| *Adagio* | At a leisurely pace, or slow |
| *Allegretto* | Quite quick, but not as quick as allegro |
| *Allegro* | Quick |
| *Andante* | At a walking pace Slower than allegretto but faster than adagio |
| *Andantino* | Sometimes a little slower than andante, but usually means a little quicker |
| *Largo* | Slow and dignified |
| *Lento* | Slow |
| *Moderato* | At a moderate speed. Neither fast nor slow |
| *Presto* | Very fast |
| *Vivace* | Lively |

**Time signature** A sign that appears after the clef and the key signature of a piece of music. It is used to show how many beats there are in each bar and what type of beats they are. For example, 3/4 means that there are three quarter notes (or crotchets) in each bar, 4/2 means that there are four half notes (or minims) in each bar.

**Tonal music** Music that is based on a major or minor key. Tonal music may modulate (move into a different key) in the middle of a piece, but it is always based on one key at a time. This is unlike bitonal music (which uses two different keys at once), polytonal music (which uses many different keys), and atonal music (which is not based on any key at all).

**Tonic** The first note (or 'keynote') of a scale.

**Transcription** A piece of music that has been changed in some way; a kind of 'arrangement'. In a transcription, the original piece may be adapted so that it can be played by different instruments from the ones the composer intended. It may also be simplified to make the music easier for a beginner to play, or made more difficult so that it can be used as a musician's showpiece.

**Transposition** A technique used to change the pitch of a piece of music. For example, a piece in the key of C major can be 'transposed' into D major by raising each of the notes by a semitone.

**Triad** A three-note chord made up of any note, plus the notes a third and a fifth above it. For example, C-E-G (the 'common chord' of C major).

**Trio** The word used to describe a composition for three voices or instruments, or the group of people who perform it. For example, the words 'piano trio' can either describe a piece of chamber music written for piano, violin and cello, or the group of three musicians who play this kind of piece.

**Triplet**   A group of three equal notes (or notes and rests), played in the time normally taken by two notes of the same length.

**Triple time**   Music that has three beats in each bar for example, 3/4 or 9/8.

**Troubadour**   Another word for minstrel. In the strictest sense, however, the troubadour was a wandering musician or poet who lived in southern France during the 1100s or 1200s.

**Twelve-note composition** A method of composing music in which all twelve notes of the chromatic scale are of equal importance.

**Twelve-note scale**   Another name for the chromatic scale.

**Unison**   A word used to describe notes that are sung or played either at the same pitch, or in octaves. If a choir sings in unison, it means that they are all singing the same tune, though the high voices (sopranos and altos) may be singing an octave higher than the low ones (tenors and basses).

**Virtuoso**   A performer who has outstanding technical ability.

**Voice**   The sound produced in humans when air passes over the vocal cords and makes them vibrate. The four most common types of singing voice are bass, tenor, alto and soprano. *Also,* a word used to describe any of the different parts or melodic lines in a contrapuntal piece such as a fugue.

**Voices**
  *Alto*   The highest adult male voice, often used in early forms of vocal music. *Also,* a shortened form of the word 'contralto'.
  *Baritone*   An adult male voice with a range higher than a bass, but lower than a tenor.
  *Bass*   The lowest male voice.
  *Contralto*   The lowest female voice, sometimes also known as an 'alto'.
  *Countertenor*   A high adult male voice, most often used in music composed before the end of the 1700s.
  *Mezzo-soprano*   A word meaning 'half soprano', used to describe a female voice that is higher than an alto but lower than a soprano.
  *Soprano*   The highest female voice. A boy with the same vocal range as a soprano is known as a 'treble'.
  *Tenor*   An adult male voice, higher than a baritone or bass, but lower than a countertenor or alto.

**Waltz**   A dance in triple time that originally appeared in Germany and Austria at the end of the 1700s. It soon developed into a graceful ballroom dance, and has remained popular ever since.

# *Index*

**The publishers would like to thank the following for supplying photographs to this book:**

**Page 10** Academia Archives *t*; **10/11** Keith Saunders *b*, Zefa *m*; **12** Mary Evans *t*; **12/13** Zefa *b*; **13** Trip *l*, LFI *t*; **14** Adrian de Groot; **15** Ancient Art and Architecture *t*, Travel Photo International *b*; **16/17** Zefa *b*; **17** Trip *r*, Zefa *t*; **18** Werner Forman *t*; **19** Robert Harding Picture Library *r*, Werner Forman *t*; **20** Holford *t*, Robert Harding Picture Library *b*; **20/21** Panos; **21** J. Allen Cash *br*, Zefa *tr*; **22** Trip; **23** Hutchison; **24** Werner Forman *t*; **24/25** Trip *b*; **25** Hutchison *t*; **26** Holford; **26/27** Hutchison; **27** Robert Harding Picture Library; **28** ET Archive *t*, Hutchison *b*; **28/29** Zefa; **29** Hutchison *t*, Ronald Grant Archive *b*; **30** © Horniman *b*, Werner Forman *t*; **30/31** Robert Harding Picture Library; **31** Zefa *b*, Robert Harding Picture Library *t*; **32** Werner Forman; **33** Robert Harding Picture Library; **34** Mary Evans *bl*, ET Archive *br*, Trinity College *t*; **34/35** Holford; **35** Mary Evans *t*; **36** Academia Archives *t*, *br*; **37** The Royal Academy of Music *b*, The Bridgeman Art Library *t*; **38** Zefa *b*, Academia Archive *t*; **39** AKG-London *t*, Reed Consumer Books *b*; **40** Wedgewood Museum *t*, AKG-London *b*; **40/41** Deutsches Theatre museum *b*, *t*; **41** © Larousse *t*; **42** The Bridgeman Art Library *l*, Mansell *b*; **42/43** The Bridgeman Art Library; **43** AKG-London; **44** Academia Archives *t*, Haags Gemeentemuseum *b*; **44/45** Mary Evans *t*, Mansell *b*; **45** Artothek; **46** Mary Evans *t*, AKG-London *b*; **46/47** Image Select; **47** AKG-London *t*, Clive Barda *b*; **48** Camera Press *b*, The Bridgeman Art Library *t*; **49** AKG-London *t*, © Schott, Performing Arts *m*, *b*; **50** Range *t*, *bl*, Aquarius *br*; **51** Redferns *t*, *b*, Bettman *m*; **52** Range *t*, Mander and Michenson *bl*; **52/53** Photofest *b*, *t*; **53** Clive Barda *br*, Zefa *tr*; **54** Range *t*, Hulton-Getty *b*; **54/55** Photofest *b*, *t*; **55** Photofest *m*; **56** Apple Corps *b*, Range *t*; **57** Redferns *l*, Rex Features *t*, LFI *r*; **58** Horniman *m*, *bl*, © Larousse *t*; **59** © Larousse; **60** © Larousse; **61** © Keith Duurders *b*, Yamaha *t*; **62** The Bridgeman Art Library *t*; **63** Zefa *t*, Redferns *m*, Robbie Jack *b*; **64** ET Archive *t*; **65** Performing Arts *br*, © Horniman *t*; **66** The Bridgeman Art Library *t*, © Horniman *b*; **66/67** © Horniman *b*, © Larousse *t*; **67** © Horniman *t*; **68** The Bridgeman Art Library *t*; **69** Hutchison *b*, Rex Features *m*, © Edinburgh *t*; **70** ET Archive *t*, Robert Harding Picture Library *m*; **70/71** © Larousse; **71** Zefa *tl*, Rex Features *tr*, © Larousse *br*; **72** The Bridgeman Art Library *t*; **73** © Larousse *br*, Redferns *t*, Topham Picture Library *m*; **74** Ann Ronan at Image Select *tl*; **75** Robert Harding *tr*, Hutchison *b*, *tl*; **76** Sonia Halliday *t*; **76/77** © Larousse; **77** Performing Arts *t*, Camera Press *b*; **78** © Larousse *r*, Sonia Halliday *t*, Range *l*; **79** Hutchison *t*, © Larousse *l*; **80** ET Archive *t*, © Horniman *b*; **81** © Laroussse *l*, © Horniman *b*, Robbie Jack *r*; **82** Sonia Halliday *t*, © Horniman *b*; **83** © Larousse *t*, Rex Features *b*; **84** Mary Evans *t*, © Larousse *m*; **84/85** © Larousse; **85** Pica Press Foto *b*, © Larousse *m*; **86** ET Archive *t*, Harrison and Harrison *b*; **87** Keith Saunders *b*, Performing Arts *tr*, Victoria and Albert *tl*; **88** Lebrecht Collection *t*; **88/89** Yamaha; **89** Robert Harding Picture Library *b*, Aquarius *tr*, Redferns *m*; **90** ET Archive; **91** Zefa *b*, ET Archive *t*, *b*; **92** © Larousse *t*, J. Allan Cash *b*; **93** Panos *tr*, Image Select *tl*; **94** Werner Forman *t*, Hutchison *t*; **95** Hutchison *t*, *b*, Magnum *br*; **96** Ancient Art and Architecture *t*, Pressens Bild *b*; **97** Hutchison *t*, Random Dance Company *r*; **98** AKG-London *t*, LFI *b*; **98/99** Redferns; **99** Performing Arts *tr*, Aquarius *tl*; **100** Hutchison *r*, Lenn Hardy of Matthew Brady *t*; **101** © Larousse *b*, Rex Features *t*; **104** AKG-London *tl*, Image Select *bl*, © Larousse *r*; **105** AKG-London *t*, Clive Barda *b*; **106** Aquarius *mr*, National Portrait Gallery *ml*, Image Select *b*; **107** AKG-London *t*, © Larousse *r*; **108** © Larousse *l*; **108/9** © Larousse *t*, Hulton-Getty *b*; **109** Hulton-Getty *t*, © Larousse *r*; **111** Mary Evans *br*; **118** © Larousse; **120** © Larousse; **121** © Larousse; **122** © Larousse; **123** © Larousse; **124** © Larousse; **125** © Larousse.

**Artists**

Harry Clow, Eugene Fleury, Chris Forsey, Pamela Goodchild (B. L. Kearley), Mark Iley, Mike Lacey (Simon Girling Assoc.), Patrick Mulrey, Darren Paterson (Garden Studio), Sebastian Quigley (Lindon Artists), Clive Spong (Linden Artists), Catherine Ward (Simon Girling Assoc.)

**The publishers would also like to thank the following for their contribution to this book:**

Claire Berridge, Margaret Birley and the Horniman Museum, Boffin Media Services, Boosey and Hawkes, Quentin Daniel, Katie Elliot, Embassy of Indonesia, Roy Flooks, Kelly Flynn, Eddie Grabham, Nina Hathaway, Honor Head, Paul Lawley, Julia March, Antony Mason, Arnold Meyer, Mel Pickering, Premiere, Janet de Saulles, Mike Sheppard and Music Sales, Professor Denis Stevens, Peter Thoms, Victor Stevenson, Dave Whitehead, The Witch Ball, Yamaha, Eleanor Van Zandt.